Around the Historic City of London

STAN JARVIS
Illustrated by David Baker

BELL & HYMAN
London

First published in 1981 by
BELL & HYMAN LIMITED
Denmark House
37-39 Queen Elizabeth Street
London SE1 2QB

British Library Cataloguing in Publication Data

Jarvis, Stanley Melville

    Around the historic City of London.
    1. London — Description — 1951

    I. Title
      914.21'2'04857   DA 679

ISBN 0 7135 1249 0

Printed in Great Britain by Fletcher & Son Ltd., Norwich

The Authors

Stan Jarvis was born in Winchester, Hampshire, in 1926. After war service in the Royal Navy, he became a student of librarianship at the City Literary Institute and has been fascinated ever since by the lore, the life and the landscapes of that famous 'Square Mile'.

His life as a librarian has taken him around the south of England and finally to Essex where he is the County's Deputy Divisional Librarian based on Chelmsford. He has published five books on Essex, including *Around Historic Essex, A View Into Essex* and *Victorian and Edwardian Essex from Old Photographs.*

David Baker gave up a career in accountancy to become a freelance artist in 1974. He specialises in pen and ink drawings.

Dedication

To my loved and loving sister
Winifred Evelyn Jarvis

Index

Victoria Embankment

Sir Christopher Wren included a new embankment of the river in his post-Fire plans for rebuilding the City, but nothing came of it. Following Sir Joseph Bazalgette's designs, and with work starting in 1864, the Embankment became a reality in 1870. A mile and a quarter of the north bank upstream from Blackfriars was rebuilt, reclaiming land from the tidal sweep behind an eight-feet-thick granite wall, beyond which a broad road was bordered on its other side by a narrow band of attractive gardens. At the City boundary here, the dragon supporting the City's arms was produced in 1849 for the London Coal Exchange, demolished in 1963. Nearby is one of the unusual seats provided for viewers of Thames traffic. They are supported by legs in the form of camels, a pleasant Egyptian conceit no doubt intended to reflect the influence of Cleopatra's Needle to the west.

The memorial to the men lost in the submarine service in two World Wars is as near the water of the national river as it can be, and most moving in its simplicity. The very decorative lamp standards proudly carry the date of completion.

The Temple

Gardens, lawyers' offices, Halls and Church make up the Temple, so called from its possession back in the twelfth century by the Order of Knights Templars, succeeded by the Knights Hospitallers of St John and ultimately leased in the fourteenth century to the fraternity of the law which still occupies it.

The chambers rising high above Inner Temple Lane form a sound barrier, making the Temple truly a peaceful place. In its gardens, legend has it, were picked the roses, red and white, which differentiated York and Lancaster. The fountain there is beautified by Margaret Wrightson's sensitive figure of a boy holding open a book with the inscription, 'Lawyers were children once', a timely reminder from the essay *Old Benchers of the Inner Temple* by Charles Lamb, to whose memory it was erected in 1930, because he was born in chambers in Crown Office Row in 1775.

A great deal of damage was done to the place in the Second World War, but the visitor standing in Fountain Court by Middle Temple Hall finds this hard to believe, restoration has been so sympathetic, so complete.

The Temple Church

The long Middle Temple Lane leads up from the Embankment through the gates of the Temple past all the bustle and intrigue of countless lawyers' chambers to the glory of their church. On the floor just a step inside the door lie the effigies of the rebel Geoffrey de Mandeville (died 1144), first Earl of Essex, and successive Earls of Pembroke who in the thirteenth century went to the Crusades, fought their battles and came home to die and be buried here in the Round Church of the Order of Knights Templars, built in 1185.

The Round Church, surprisingly, is new. The fire which consumed the old one on 10 May 1941, the last night of the Blitz, was so intense that even the marble pillars were split apart. A tablet records the gratitude of the 'Honourable Societies of the Inner and Middle Temple to Walter Hindes Godfrey and his son Walter Emil Godfrey for their skill in restoration . . .' and to those who worked with them on this thirteen-year-long task. The Round Church had a magnificent 'choir' added in 1240, which has also been restored with the most colourful great east windows, and rededicated in 1954.

Temple Bar

A bar or gate of some kind had protected access to the
City from the west ever since the twelfth century. In
medieval times the spikes on top of the gate sported the
heads of executed criminals. 'Temple Bar,' we are told,
'marked a bound which no English King was allowed to
pass without the Lord Mayor's consent. Not until that
worthy had handed his sword to the monarch and the
latter had returned it was he free to enter the city . . .
The ancient custom obtains to this day.' (*The Wonderful Story of London*).

The gateway was given added significance by Wren's
fine rebuilding of 1672 in Portland stone, which
included pedestrian arches each side of a broad road
arch over which, in niches, were placed statues of
Charles I and II in Roman costume and of James I and,
it is thought, Queen Elizabeth. In 1746, Horace
Walpole recalled, people with spy-glasses were charging a halfpenny a look at 'the new heads on Temple
Bar'. It stayed until 1878 when it must have been
causing great traffic problems and was becoming
unsafe. After it was taken down, its stones grew moss in
Plumstead Marshes until they were later re-assembled
as the entrance to Theobalds Park, near Cheshunt, in
Hertfordshire.

corca 1760

Temple Bar

The most exact definition of the city boundary must surely be found in the middle of the road where the Strand gives way to Fleet Street. Here, on the memorial to the old Temple Bar, an inscription explains that the centre line from west to east through the former gateway passed three feet ten inches south of an arrow engraved below.

The larger letters around the top of the plinth tell us: 'Temple Bar formerly stood here, 1880.' Above them rears up the bronze dragon, supporter of the City arms, while on the east and west sides of the column stand images of Queen Victoria and the Prince of Wales, later Edward VII. The south side shows, in miniature, the progress of the Queen to the Guildhall on 9 November 1837. The crowd of tiny figures in blackened bronze is an absorbing study. One little figure has engraved upon his back, 'Edward our Founder; Victoria our Friend' — a hopeful heart-cry from the City Fathers! On the north side similar figures act out the scene of the Queen's procession to St Paul's on 27 February 1872.

It is a pity that the density of today's traffic prevents many pedestrians from approaching closely enough to appreciate the fascinating detail of J. E. Boehm's design.

St Dunstan-in-the-West

Though the gates were firmly locked on our last visit there is much to see without forcing one's way into the 'spacious vaulted octagon' which was built by John Shaw in 1833 and much restored in 1950. By the side gate one can slip into the churchyard and see, over the vestry porch, the only statue of Queen Elizabeth I carved while she was still alive. It was originally placed on the west side of the Lud Gate when it was built in 1586 and only presented to the church when the gate was demolished in 1760. The Queen looks down on legendary King Lud and his two sons who once enjoyed equality with her on that gate. Today they stand in the porch behind a grille which makes them look like prisoners of war but defeats vandals.

From the street there is a grand view of the unusual clock made in 1671, with two wooden 'giants' to strike the quarters and the hours on bells in a kind of temple made of wood. The clock itself stands out over the street on a long bracket. This wonderful mechanism was removed when the church was being rebuilt in 1832, and sold to the Marquis of Hertford for his house in Regent's Park, where it stayed until 1935, when, through the generosity of Lord Rothermere, it was returned to its rightful place.

Fleet Street

The fact that national newspapers have their offices here gives the street an atmosphere of tension and bustle. Geoffrey Fletcher, in his *City Sights* says, '... A properly constituted human being with all faculties in equilibrium ought to feel at his best in Fleet Street ... one of the most fascinating streets in any city known to me ...'

It is named from the Fleet River which once ran down the middle of this thoroughfare in an open ditch, acting as a sewer for the close-packed population which lived in the most primitive conditions. The river became such a health hazard that in 1764 it was arched over and so became a sewer in reality. The original Fleet River rose at Hampstead and ran through Hockley-in-the-Hole to Saffron Hill, joining, thereabouts, the Hole Bourne from which Holborn gets its name. After passing along what is now Farringdon Street and New Bridge Street, it joined the Thames at Blackfriars.

It was on the site of no. 1, Fleet Street that the Devil Tavern stood when Ben Jonson was a giant among pygmies at the Apollo Club there. From 1671 it has been Child's Bank, now incorporated in Williams and Glyn, and its records include the signatures of well-known people as different as Oliver Cromwell and Nell Gwynne.

Johnson's House

Although Boswell faithfully recorded sixteen houses in London in which Dr Samuel Johnson (1709-1784) lived at one time or another, only the house in Gough Square has survived. This is the place where he dwelt from 1748 to 1759. In the long room at the top of the house the famous dictionary was compiled and here also Johnson wrote *Rasselas* as well as his contributions to *The Rambler* and *The Idler*. He first met Boswell in 1736, so visitors today tread in the footsteps of the great man and his biographer, for Johnson said in the parting at dawn after that first meeting, 'Sir, I am glad we have met. I hope we shall pass many evenings and mornings too, together.' We know they did, and therefore Boswell must have climbed the steps to Number 17, Gough Square many times.

The house itself was built around 1700, was considerably restored in 1948 and is open on weekdays to the public for a small fee. It was Johnson who wrote, '. . . when a man is tired of London, he is tired of life; for there is in London all that life can afford.'

Wine Office Court

From the hustle of the newspaper world, represented by the looming offices of the *Daily Telegraph*, designed by Elcock and Sutcliffe in 1930, one can step into nearby Wine Office Court, an alleyway into history. Not a quiet alleyway, however, for the Wine Office Restaurant and the Cheshire Cheese draw tourists as a magnet attracts iron filings. Many of these hurrying sightseers miss the writing on the wall which does so add to the appreciation of this narrow passage:

'This Court takes its name from the Excise Office which was here up to 1665. Voltaire came and, says tradition, Congreve and Pope. Dr Johnson lived in Gough Square (end of Court, on the left), and finished his Great Dictionary there in 1755. Oliver Goldsmith lived at No. 6, where he partly wrote *The Vicar of Wakefield* and Johnson saved him from eviction by selling the book for him. Here came Johnson's friends, Reynolds, Gibbon, Garrick, Dr Burney, Boswell and others of his circle. In the nineteenth century came Carlyle, Macaulay, Tennyson, Dickens (who mentions the Court in *A Tale of Two Cities*), Forster, Hood, Thackeray, Cruikshank, Leech and Wilkie Collins . . . '

'Sir,' said Dr Johnson, 'If you wish to have a just notion of the magnitude of this great City you must not be satisfied with seeing its great streets and squares but must survey the innumerable little lanes and courts . . . ' How true of this Court!

Ye Olde Cheshire Cheese

There is a step in the City of London so worn away by constant pilgrimage that is has had to be protected by a metal grating. It is the threshold of the Cheshire Cheese in Wine Office Court, off Fleet Street. Newspaper men and women and tourists fight for attention in the sand-strewn bars which have been furnished and decorated to preserve the atmosphere of its rebuilding in 1667. The great Dr Johnson came to this tavern, so it is natural that a chair which he is said to have owned is on permanent display.

The Chop Bar and Restaurant are very popular, deservedly so from the historical point of view, for this is the only one of the old taverns now in existence in Fleet Street, as proudly proclaimed in the wordy notice on the wall which once saw the light of the great oil lantern which still overhangs the door: 'Ye Olde Cheshire Cheese. Rebuilt 1667 in the reign of Charles II and continued successively under 15 Sovereigns . . .' Though the notice claims that Dr Johnson and his biographer Boswell were regular patrons, the place gets no mention in the famous *Life*.

Salisbury Court

Opposite Shoe Lane off Fleet Street is the sign for Salisbury Court. Unremarkable in its architecture today, this lane must be remembered for the famous man who was born here, on 23 February 1633, on the site of the White Swan, and baptised in nearby St Bride's. Samuel Pepys, son of a tailor, left Cambridge University to become secretary to a rich relative, Sir Edward Montagu, who continued as his patron. Samuel began his diary on 1 January 1660. From that day on we have a fascinating first-hand account of how he went, '. . . to every play, to every execution, to every procession, fire, concert, riot, trial, review, city feast, and picture gallery, that he can hear of . . .' (Lord Jeffrey). His record of the splendour of Restoration life in London is followed by the panic years of plague and fire.

Sad to say, Pepys's sight began to fail as early as 1664. By 1669 he was compelled to record, 'And thus ends all that I doubt I shall ever be able to do with my own eyes in the keeping of my Journall . . .' But he did not go blind. He lived on for another twenty years and died in 1703, to be buried beside his wife in St Olave's Church. That precious, unique diary, in cipher, stayed in manuscript at Magdalene College, Cambridge, until 1825, when it was deciphered by John Smith and edited for publication by Lord Braybrooke.

THE CORPORATION OF
IN A HOUSE ON THIS SITE
SAMUEL PEPYS
DIARIST
WAS BORN
1632 – 1703
THE CITY OF LONDON

16

St Bride's Church

Sir John Betjeman has described the steeple, rising to a height of 226 feet, ' . . . of diminishing octagons, ending in a spirelet, [it] is like a ring of bells'. A more prosaic baker, William Rich (1755-1811), looking from his window at 3 Ludgate Hill, decided that it was an excellent model for a many-tiered wedding cake, and so started the fashion of iced elegance which still takes pride of place at the reception. Though it is really but a shortened form of Bridget, what name of a church could be more appropriate for such a model?

The church that stood on this site before the Fire saw the baptism of Samuel Pepys in 1633. The present church, so beautifully built by Wren in 1680, was seriously damaged in the Second World War, but that wonderful steeple survived, shorter by eight feet than the original because it was struck by lightning in 1764 and had to be rebuilt. Now the interior has been splendidly restored, using Wren's original plans with one or two interesting modifications by the architect Godfrey Allen.

Before this extensive rebuilding, excavation of the old church floor showed evidence of seven churches erected here right back to the eleventh century. Saxon and then Roman and earlier levels yielded evidence of burials on an unprecedented scale. Two thousand of the 5,000 unidentified skeletons discovered were removed to Cambridge University for a three-year period of research.

In the present crypt in 1969 Sir Max Aitken paid for a permanent display of the finds on the site, as a memorial to his father Lord Beaverbrook. Of the many fascinating exhibits from this small square of ground we can smile at the remnant of wedding dress worn by Susannah when she married that same William Rich, who no doubt modelled the steeple once again on the wedding cake.

St Bride Foundation Institute

Amid the historic grandeur of the City it is a real pleasure to encounter the late Victorian earnestness of the St Bride Foundation Institute with its typically institutional architecture and its stairs and passageways leading to halls, lecture rooms, and library originally founded for printers. Climb two flights of stairs and pause for a rest beside the office where you can read the foundation stone — if it can still be called that — on the first floor: 'St Bride Foundation Institute. To commemorate the erection of this building this stone was laid by H.R.H. Albert Edward, Prince of Wales, K.G., on the 20th day of November 1893.'

Today it provides courses as varied as ballroom dancing and table tennis, photography and billiards for anybody living or working between the Bank and Temple Bar, and the St Bride Printing Library is a public reference library of some 30,000 books, pamphlets and periodicals on printing and typography. A permanent exhibition of the history of typography is being planned.

Blackfriars Bridge

Bridges are a blessing for everybody, except the ferryman! When Blackfriars Bridge was completed to Robert Mylne's design in 1769, the management committee had to compensate the Watermen's Company to the tune of nearly £14,000 for the loss to them of the Sunday ferry alone. The toll for use of the bridge was a halfpenny on weekdays and a penny on Sundays until it was redeemed in 1785.

The Common Council decided it should be called Pitt Bridge after the great statesman who resigned from office in 1768, but association in the popular mind with the ancient monastery on the site where the bridge connected with the north bank of the Thames caused that name to be dropped in favour of Blackfriars.

After a century of use, and in conjunction with the construction of the Victoria Embankment, the bridge was rebuilt with iron arches on stone piers, designed by Sir Joseph Cubitt and opened by Queen Victoria on 6 November 1869. In 1908 it was widened from 70 to 105 feet to accommodate tramways, thus making it the widest bridge over the Thames.

St Andrew-by-the-Wardrobe

Though it sounds like a ghostly visitation, this is a church in Queen Victoria Steet near which there once stood the King's Great Wardrobe. The church was rebuilt after the Fire by Sir Christopher Wren and finished in 1692, but a second fiery attack in the Second World War destroyed his work. It was restored once again, under the direction of Marshall Sisson, by 1961, using some furniture and features rescued from other bombed-out churches. A simple, yet dignified, red-brick building with a plain tower, it has an unusual and attractive ceiling.

The connection with the Wardrobe is explained by Sir Walter Besant in his *Survey of the City of London*: 'On the north side of St Andrew's church stands a small square which, with its trees and the absence of vehicles or shops, is one of the most quiet spots in the whole City. This square was formerly the court of the town house built by Sir John Beauchamp (died 1539) whose tomb in St Paul's Cathedral was commonly called Duke Humphrey's tomb. Before his death the house became the property of King Edward III, who made it a Royal Wardrobe House and so it remained until the Great Fire. James I gave the collection of dresses . . . to the Earl of Dunbar, by whom they were all sold and dispersed . . . '

Apothecaries' Hall

What a transformation it is to step from the present-day bustle of Blackfriars Lane through the pillared entrance stairway into the eighteenth-century environment of the courtyard of Apothecaries' Hall. Beside the main door there is a memorial in the form of a huge, old leaden cistern embossed 'Laboratory stock 1786' with an accompanying tablet which tells us the Hall was repaired in 1967 to celebrate the 350th anniversary of the foundation of the Society of Apothecaries in 1617 with a charter from James I.

The land on which it stands was bought by the Society in 1632 but the buildings are post-Great Fire and further restored in 1786, as witness that cistern. Whilst the wings are given over to offices, the Great Hall is on the first floor of the main block. At its south end is a bust of Gideon de Laune, founder of the Society, which, we are reminded, 'To this day . . . remains a craft guild, but the apothecary is recognised by the state as a fully qualified medical practitioner.' He has come a long way since Dryden (1631-1700) wrote:

> The apothecary tribe is wholly blind;
>
> From files a random recipe they take,
>
> And many deaths from one prescription make . . .

But Dryden supported the College of Physicians in their opposition to the Society competing with them in the making of medicine. So he was not unbiased.

St Benet's Church

For over a hundred years now the Welsh Episcopalians have claimed this as their special church. In former days its north aisle was filled with ecclesiastical lawyers and heralds from the Doctors' Commons and the College of Arms on the other side of Queen Victoria Street. They paced the same old stone floor as we do and, by the beautifully-lettered slate memorials let into it, worshippers down the ages have been reminded of the transitory nature of life on earth.

The church had to be rebuilt by Sir Christopher Wren between 1677 and 1685 after the Fire and was again much damaged when set on fire by an arsonist in 1971. But it looks just the same from the outside as it did when Henry Fielding walked in past the walls of red brick chequered with white stone at the corners, the long rounded windows with decorative festoons above, to marry here for the second time in 1747.

It is also worth remembering that in the former church was buried Inigo Jones (1573-1652), the theatrical designer and first great English architect, who laid out Covent Garden and Lincoln's Inn Fields and built the Queen's House at Greenwich.

College of Arms

The buildings bordering Queen Victoria Street have altered much since it was opened in 1871, but the College of Arms continues on the site vested in it in 1555 when Queen Mary confirmed their charter received from Richard III in 1484. The Fire of 1666 destroyed the College but by 1671 it had risen again, in brick, under the supervising eye of Francis Sandford, the Lancaster Herald, to the design of Maurice Emmett. And so we see it today, though it was thoroughly restored in 1956, when the grand eighteenth century wrought-iron gates, formerly at Goodrich Court, Hertfordshire, were presented by an American well-wisher.

The entrance hall is crowded with heraldic devices, banners and portraits of great men in the College. Here one waits to see, by appointment, the three Kings of Arms, six Heralds of Arms and four Pursuivants of Arms who help the Earl Marshal in the arrangement of great state ceremonies and daily delve into and confirm pedigrees and the right to bear arms, using a library unequalled in the world in its coverage of heraldry, genealogy and allied subjects.

The Bell, Carter Lane

Thank goodness the names of streets last longer than the buildings which line them! Time and again they give us the vital clue to the history of the locality. Carter Lane, for example, reminds us that Carters like the brothers le Charetter, living here as long ago as 1319, could be hired for work in this area.

Now Faraday Buildings, home of the Post Office telephone service, spreads its huge block along that street, but the little lane which gives access to its inner depths is still called Bell Yard, a lingering relic of the days of the busy Bell Tavern, sufficiently famous to have a plaque on the wall: 'Upon this site formerly stood The Bell, Carter Lane, from whence Richard Quiney wrote the letter to William Shakespeare dated 25th October 1598. This is the only letter extant addressed to Shakespeare and the original is preserved in the museum at his birthplace, Stratford-upon-Avon. This tablet was placed upon the present building by leave of the Postmaster General. 1899.'

Painters' Hall

The exterior is not remarkable, but step inside and the glory of this house of the Painters and Stainers is clear to see. Naturally its standard of decoration must be of the highest order and this is proved, beautifully, in the Painted Chamber, which has been restored and decorated with the original painted panels. Sir John Browne, Serjeant-painter to Henry VIII, gave his house in Little Trinity Lane to the Company in 1532 and this has been the site of their Hall ever since. The Great Fire consumed it, but in 1670 it was rebuilt and carefully maintained over the centuries only to be burnt down again through enemy action in 1941. Twenty years passed before it could be opened again on the site now extended to Huggin Hill.

Interesting connections with times past are the oak carvings in the entrance hall and the marble bust of Thomas Evans in the Court Room, all done by Edward Pearce, Master of the Company in 1693. The Painters were well organized in the thirteenth century and the Stainers, originating probably as painters on woven fabric, were developing as a separate body. In 1502 their petition for union was granted by the Lord Mayor, though they had to wait until 1575 before achieving a charter of incorporation as a Livery Company.

Beaver House

Great and Little Trinity Lanes, together with Garlick Hill, define the limits of Beaver House, Headquarters of the Hudson's Bay Company which, by its royal charter of 1670, was granted ownership of and trading monopoly throughout all the lands which drained into Canada's Hudson Bay. For two centuries the trappers brought their hard-won pelts to the Hudson's Bay store for transformation into those fabulous furs for London ladies. Then, in 1870, the Company exchanged its vast holdings for fairer farming land on the Prairie, courtesy of the Canadian government. But the trading posts continued, developed into general stores and today form a long chain of department stores throughout Canada.

However the Company still deals in furs, but on a consignment sales basis. The City of London guide explains, 'In Beaver House, London, the company's fur sales organisation handles for sale . . . 56 different kinds of fur ranging from tiny moleskins from Scotland to tigers from China . . . and — with its historic link to the company's earliest beginning — beaver.' Beaver House, built in 1926, and also housing the London Fur Exchange, has over its entrance a carving of a beaver and a sailing ship among the ice floes, the pivots of their prosperity.

Vintners' Hall

Visitors to Vintners' Hall in Upper Thames Street, just west of Queen Street Place, are referred to Kennet Wharf Place, where the Clerk's offices are in a sumptuous modern block in striking contrast to the ancient foundation of the Company in 1364, when its charter allowed it a monopoly of trade with Gascony. The increasingly important Company achieved incorporation in 1437 but fell on hard times from 1553, when its right to sell wine was curtailed, through to Puritan times a century later when another setback came in the form of the Great Fire which practically destroyed the Hall and much other property. Yet the Vinters survived and with a new charter granted on 20 August 1973 the Company is again making an impact on the wine trade.

Their Hall was rebuilt in 1671 but the Company faced another crisis when the widening of Upper Thames Street in 1822 lopped off its front rooms. The Court Room remained and is one of the oldest rooms in London, having been built in 1446 and having survived the Fire. Some lovely eighteenth-century pieces are included amongst its furniture. The façade and entrance were renewed in 1910. The Hall escaped the hazards of two World Wars, to be carefully restored in recent times when some of the unnecessary Victorian embellishments were removed.

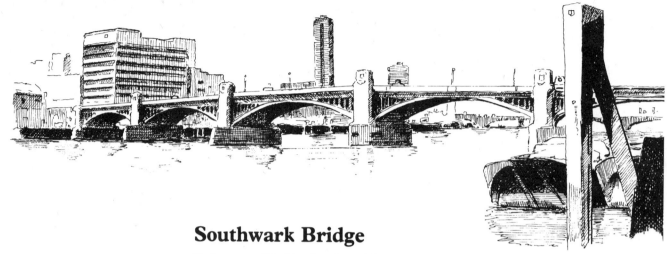

Southwark Bridge

Built as a toll bridge by the celebrated John Rennie between 1813 and 1819 for a private company which hoped to recoup its outlay and make a profit, Southwark Bridge was opened on 24 March 1819, just as the St Paul's clock struck midnight. It had the modern innovation of stairs leading from the middle of the west side down to a steam-boat pier. The scheme was very successful and continued until 1865 when an Act of Parliament ordered its transfer to the Corporation for around a quarter of a million pounds. This was effected in 1868 and the toll was abolished.

Early in the twentieth century plans were put in hand to reconstruct the bridge and its approaches. Building began in 1913 but was held up by the First World War and so was not completed to Sir Ernest George's designs until 1921, when it was opened by King George V. It is a very good vantage point for viewing the Thames and its traffic as well as bankside buildings. To the east is the railway bridge to Cannon Street Station and to the west the rail and road bridges to Blackfriars.

St Michael, Paternoster Royal

Only the walls and tower remained after an air raid in 1944. In the ruins a mummified cat was found, thought to have been a live sacrifice made by Wren's workmen when they rebuilt the old church after its destruction in the Great Fire. Having been restored once again and re-dedicated in 1968, it now serves as the chapel and central office of the Missions to Seamen.

The windows by John Hayward are particularly fine. There is one on the south side which shows that familiar figure of a youth striding along with a stick over his shoulder to which is tied a large handkerchief containing all his worldly goods — Dick Whittington, of course. His cat may have been legendary but he was real, rich and very charitable, repairing many public buildings in the City including this church, next door to which, in 1422, he built himself a fine house. Its foundations form the cellars of the present Whittington Wine Bar. He died the following year and was buried beside his wife under a costly monument which unfortunately did not survive that first holocaust of 1666.

Skinners' Hall

On Dowgate Hill opposite Cannon Street station stands Skinners' Hall; its imposing entrance at no. 8 is somewhat upstaged by similar portals at nos. 4 and 10 to the Tallow Chandlers' and Dyers' Halls respectively. In order of precedence among Livery Companies, the Skinners rank sixth and seventh in alternate years, along with the Merchant Taylors, due to some controversy lost in history. The splendour of their procession on Corpus Christi day is now but a memory — 200 torchbearers with their waxen brands painted and gilded, 200 priests and choristers in ecclesiastical garb, the Mayor and Aldermen, representatives of the law and the Master and members of the Company all proceeding to church. Such pomp and panoply have gone, but the Company continues. Its first charter was granted in 1327 and through all the years up to the eighteenth century the Skinners controlled the trade in skins and furs.

Their Hall, which was in existence before 1295, was ruined in the Great Fire, rebuilt in 1670 and given a new façade in 1790. One of its treasured possessions is relatively modern — a set of fifteen panels painted by Sir Frank Brangwyn, R.A., (1867-1956) which illustrates the history and the accomplishments of the Skinners.

Fishmongers' Hall

The official guide to the City tells us: ' . . . the Fishmongers, a very rich and dignified company of which many distinguished people have been made freemen, are still empowered to seize unsound fish, an article in medieval days more productive than any other of disputes between vendor and customer.' Their Hall was the first of the City Halls to be burnt down in the Great Fire and was again the first to be set alight and badly damaged in the Second World War.

It stands at the northern end of London Bridge, presenting to the riverside the classical façade created by Henry Roberts and Gilbert Scott in 1834 and subsequently restored with the embellishment of the figures in stone, of a fisherman and woman. The interior, restored to its original grandeur, includes on the stairway the old, painted wooden statue of William Walworth, the Lord Mayor who rode out with young King Richard II in 1381 and slew the rebel leader Wat Tyler; and also the portrait of Her Majesty Queen Elizabeth II painted in 1955 by Annigoni, which has been reproduced on stamps and banknotes.

London Bridge

'... my favourite lounging-place in the interval was old London Bridge, where I was wont to sit in one of the stone recesses, watching the people going by, or to look over the balustrades at the sun shining in the water ...' says David Copperfield. No admirer of Dickens can follow in our hero's footsteps for that bridge was falling down when Dickens was born in 1812. By 1831 it had been replaced by John Rennie's famous bridge, built with the assistance of his two sons. Although London Bridge had been reconstructed in 1763, it was still the same stone bridge Peter Colechurch started building in 1176, which was not finished until 1209. The houses and the chapel of St Thomas Becket which turned it into a narrow street were demolished after fire ravaged them in 1758.

The present bridge was built between 1967 and 1973 without once stopping the flow of traffic, calculated at 3,000 vehicles and 20,000 pedestrians during the rush hour. Rennie's bridge was removed in 1972 in the form of 10,000 granite slabs, individually marked, to the booming new town of Lake Havasu City in Arizona. There it was re-erected across the neck of a great artificial lake to connect the city with its airport.

The Monument

As if it was the only monument in the City, or in the world for that matter, the Monument is called just that by everybody. Even the underground railway station is named after it in the same imperial manner. It was built, under an Act of Parliament, 'in perpetual remembrance' not so much of the ravages of the Great Fire of 1666 as of the remarkable speed of the rebuilding that followed it.

Naturally it was planned by Sir Christopher Wren, in association with Robert Hook, the City surveyor. Wren's idea was for a smooth column with flames in gilt bronze erupting at intervals up it to be surmounted by a great flaming urn and crowned with a phoenix, wings outspread, rising from it. In the six years it took to build it, from 1676 on, the plan was varied. The phoenix, perched at the top of the column with its 345-step black marble internal staircase, had to be omitted because of the problem of stability at 202 feet above the ground, and the column was fluted in the Doric fashion.

This curious height was chosen because the Monument was sited just that distance away from the baker's shop in Pudding Lane where the fire broke out. The plinth is decorated with bas-reliefs by C. G. Cibber which represent the City mourning over its ruins with Time giving her support and the Angels of Peace and Plenty hovering helpfully above. Charles II, in Roman costume, commands the services of Science, Architecture and Liberty.

From the balcony, at the top of all those steps, there is a magnificent view. It is caged with iron, to the detriment of its appearance, because it was such a popular place for suicides in Victorian times.

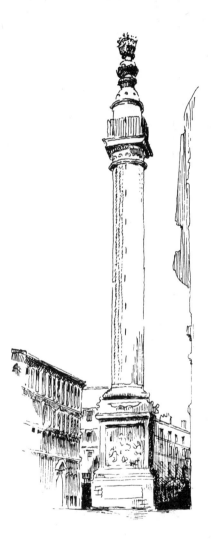

Billingsgate

'You're no better than a Billingsgate fish-fag,' said our great-grandmothers if any one in the family shouted, argued, or used bad language. 'Talking Billingsgate', again, implied swearing, so the fish market has much to answer for, but over the last century it has lived down that reputation. The Billings are said to have been of the same ancient British people as the Varini mentioned by Tacitus, and it appears that the Romans gave their name to the area where they inserted a gate in their wall giving onto the river.

Today more than a hundred firms employ some 2,500 people in the great wholesale fish market here, handling close on 400 tons of fish in three hours each day, in a place which has a history going back to the earliest written records around 1400. Billingsgate Wharf is thought to have been used for landing fish for sale to growing London town as early as the ninth century, though it is no longer used for the purpose. The only observable connection with earlier days is in the leather-and-wood hats worn by some of the porters to enable them to carry on their heads up to a hundredweight of fish at a time. But the wind of change blows even here. There is a plan to move Billingsgate to the dockland area because it is hindering road development.

Custom House

From London Bridge or from the deck of H.M.S. *Belfast* one gets the best view of the London Port Collection building of the Board of Customs and Excise. The Custom House, adjoining Billingsgate market, has a 490-feet frontage to the Thames along Custom House Wharf. It is an historic site, used for the same purpose from way back in the fourteenth century. The present building was erected between 1814 and 1817 to designs by David Laing, but unfortunately the foundations failed to support the middle section, so that part had to be rebuilt to plans by Sir Robert Smirke in 1828. It is the sixth Custom House to be built on this spot.

On the quay which fronts it, William Cowper the poet (1731-1800) is said to have dallied in despair, contemplating suicide by leaping into the Thames, during a severe mental breakdown. He resisted the impulse and recovered to produce not only his brilliant poetry but also the 'Olney Hymns' in co-operation with that slave-trader-turned-minister John Newton who became rector of St Mary Woolnoth from 1780.

Let another famous citizen have the last word. Dr Johnson in his *Dictionary* declares: 'EXCISE. A hateful tax levied upon commodities, and adjudged not by the common judges of property, but wretches hired by those to whom excise is paid.'

St Dunstan-in-the-East

This church, just a step from the Thames, off St Dunstan's Hill, must have a place in any book on the City because it was the last church to be built by Sir Christopher Wren after the Great Fire, with a beautiful slender spire supported by flying buttresses on a tower completed by 1702 — 'his most airy and elegant Gothic work' (Sir John Betjeman).

That tower is the only evidence of his work remaining, for the rest of the church was rebuilt to David Laing's design from 1817 to 1821 and that charming 'Georgian Perpendicular' rebuilding was gutted by enemy action in 1941. But within the battered walls the Worshipful Company of Gardeners has planned and planted a beautiful garden. On the outside of the south wall there survives a fig tree planted in 1937 to commemorate the coronation of George VI.

One celebrated person buried in the old church is Sir John Hawkins, admiral and sea rover under Queen Elizabeth. Now the nearest one can come to a sense of his presence is in the bubbling of the fountain which makes the garden specially attractive on a summer's morning.

Bakers' Hall

That baking was a recognised craft as early as the twelfth century is proved by entries in the Exchequer accounts which show the Bakers paying a yearly sum to the King for the privilege of levying their own taxes. The first charter granted to a guild of bakers is dated 1486, with renewal and confirmation in 1569 and 1685. The Assize of Bread was the important control of quality and quantity. It is said that the thirteen of the 'Baker's dozen' was an early assurance against short weight.

The Company's second Hall, built in Harp Lane, was burnt down in the Great Fire; rough justice this, for the fire started in a baker's shop. In 1715 their third Hall was burnt down again — and yet again in 1940 when it was bombed. So the new hall designed by Trehearne and Norman Preston and Partners in 1963 is the fourth hall on the same site. Its windows, designed by John Piper, commemorate the burning of those former halls.

The Tower of London

Since the official guide to the City of London does itself say that the Tower, '. . . is not actually within the City but can hardly be omitted here,' we feel fully justified in included it in *our* book. After all, it was first built to impress and subdue those unruly, individualistic Citizens by William the Conqueror, who set in hand the White Tower, oldest part of the great fortification. Under Henry III (1216-72) this modest castle, with the Tower as the Keep, was turned into a powerful fortress. Edward I added the outer 'curtain' and excavated the moat around it over ten years from 1275. Its defences have never really been put to the test for its history is more of imprisonment and execution than siege and assault.

The sad catalogue runs from the execution of Sir William Wallace in 1305 and includes that of Henry VI in 1471 and those 'little Princes in the Tower', Edward V and his brother, somewhere around 1483. Anne Boleyn, married here in pomp and ceremony to Henry VIII, was cruelly beheaded in the same place in 1536. Down in the dungeons Guy Fawkes and his conspirators were tortured into confession. Simon, Lord Lovat was the last person to be beheaded here, in 1747, for his part in the second Jacobite rebellion, but the last people to die here were the spies caught in two World Wars.

The Tower of London

The place which attracts more queues of the curious than any other City sight must surely be the West End of Waterloo Barracks, built in 1845 within the Tower, where the Crown Jewels are now placed permanently on show in a special vault. In the ground floor room above it one can see the Great Sword of State made in 1678 and used at each Opening of Parliament, the robes of the monarch worn at coronations since 1821, and the insignia of the Orders of Knighthood.

The Crown Jewels in that vault are not all that old because during the Commonwealth the ancient symbols of monarchy were done away with. The oldest crown on view is St Edward's Crown, weighing five pounds, honouring Edward the Confessor and made of gold for the coronation of Charles II in 1661. It is still used at every coronation ceremony, being replaced by the Imperial State Crown made for Queen Victoria in 1838 and set with over three thousand jewels. The Imperial Indian Crown boasts over 1,000 diamonds. It was worn by George V in 1911 at the great Delhi Durbar. When his Queen was crowned in the same year she wore the crown set with the famous Koh-i-Noor diamond. This wonderful collection includes orbs, sceptres, maces, bracelets, swords, anointing spoon and ampula.

The Tower of London

What does an elephant wear in wartime? Only in the New Armouries of the Tower of London can this question be answered. The suit of elephant's armour there displayed was probably brought back from the Battle of Plassey, won by Clive of India in 1757. But that is just a novelty in a wide-ranging collection of armour, weapons and firearms covering the eighteenth and nineteenth centuries and supplemented by armour from the Royal Collections.

The New Armouries back on to the wall between Broad Arrow Tower and Salt Tower, all thirteenth-century work. In the Salt Tower one's heart goes out to those prisoners, long since out of their misery, whose pathetic carvings in the stone include a diagram for casting horoscopes cut out by someone in 1561 who evidently had a lot of time on his hands. It is thought that the tower derived its name from the gunpowder and saltpetre once stored here.

North of the Armouries is the Regimental Museum of the Royal Fusiliers (City of London Regiment) which was formed in the Tower in 1685 and amalgamated with others in 1968. Those Fusiliers would have guarded the gate when a password, or 'by-word', was a very necessary preliminary to entry by the privileged. Today tourists enter under the Byward (by-word) Tower in their thousands daily.

The Tower of London

In medieval times those who challenged the power of the throne and who conspired against the state were taken into the Tower, and imprisonment, via the Traitors' Gate, in a barge or boat floating in from the Thames under the sixty-feet-wide arch. Now the river has been pushed away, but it lapped at the Gate beneath the turreted St Thomas's Tower when they were both built around 1242 for King Henry III who also, it is thought, set in hand the Bloody Tower opposite, which was completed under Edward I. Here were incarcerated Thomas Cranmer, Archbishop of Canterbury, burned in 1556, Sir Walter Raleigh, who wrote his unfinished *History of the World* here in 1614, and the 'infamous Jeffreys', judge of the 'Bloody Assize' who on 18 April 1689 died in delirium on this spot.

In the White Tower is the oldest church in London, the Chapel of St John, superb in the powerful simplicity of its Norman architecture. When monarchs dwelt in the Tower this was their private chapel.

Tower Bridge

'Once considered a miracle of hydraulic engineering, the machinery of Tower Bridge has now been electrified, and the bascules rarely open because so few large ships now venture this far up the river.' (J. K. Fisher, *City of London Past and Present*.) Tower Bridge was started in 1886 and finished some four years behind schedule in 1894 at a cost of one and a half million pounds.

The massive towers needed to support the raised halves of the bridge, each weighing a thousand tons, rise 120 feet from the piers and the high-level pedestrian bridges between them are 142 feet above high water mark. They are closed these days, some say because too many people climbed all those stairs to leap to their death, but since the main roadway can be raised in just one and a half minutes, and even allowing time for the ship to pass through, it may still be quicker, and certainly less breathtaking, to wait at the barriers than to go up, over and down again.

Designers of the bridge were Sir Horace Jones, the City Architect, who died just as the work began, and Sir John Wolfe Barry, who took over with the help of the son of the famous Isambard Kingdom Brunel.

Tower Hill

When I was a student at the City Literary Institute over thirty years ago I went to Tower Hill to hear the lunchtime orators and watch the man who could tear a telephone directory in two with his bare hands. In those days I had no sense of history and viewed only with passing curiosity that little plot of ground, specially enclosed, where, as a tablet tells us, the old, the dreadful scaffold claimed the lives of so many men and women eminent in English history. It was removed about the middle of the eighteenth century, the last person to be beheaded on it (or anywhere else in Britain for that matter), being Simon, Lord Lovat who was put to death on 9 April 1747.

More than a hundred years before him Sir Thomas More suffered the same fate and, according to Roper's 'Life . . .': 'found the scaffold so rickety that he said to the officer in charge, "I pray you Master Lieutenant, see me safe up, and for my coming down let me shift for myself." ' The succession of victims of the executioner is too long to detail, but it includes at least 75 famous and unfortunate men and women branded as traitors, from Sir Simon Burley in 1388 down to Lord Lovat.

All Hallows-by-the-Tower

This church's position is made clear by its name. It stands where Great Tower Street and Byward Street meet. All Hallows — that is, All Saints, from the Old English 'halig' — one who is holy — was completely gutted in 1941 when an enemy attack destroyed even the stout Norman pillars, leaving standing only the outer walls of the fifteenth century and the seventeenth century tower of brick from which Pepys watched the previous great conflagration of 1666.

The devastation revealed evidence of a seventh-century Saxon church, a satellite of Barking Abbey. It was completely rebuilt by 1957 under the architectural direction of the late Lord Mottistone and Paul Paget, who added a spire to that tower because it had become so much more prominent in the altered skyline. Some tombs and brasses have survived, and another point of interest is the font literally hewn from the Rock of Gibraltar.

Perhaps the most important thing about this church is the fact that it is the world centre of 'Toc H', the brotherhood born of the comradeship of the First World War, founded by Padre P. B. ('Tubby') Clayton who became Vicar. Here burns the Toc H Lamp of Maintenance from which were lit all those other lamps of friendship which still shine around the world.

Trinity House

The Corporation of Trinity House started out as an association of self-help formed by mariners, which as the 'Guild, Fraternity or Brotherhood of the Most Glorious and Undivided Trinity' received its charter in 1514. Its origin is lost in time, some say as far back as King Alfred. Its location was in Deptford as shown by the 1547 confirmation of the charter to the 'Corporation of Trinity House of Deptford Strand'.

Development of trade by sea increased its power and its responsibilities in charting and marking the hazards facing shipping around the British Isles. Its income was, and is, principally derived from dues paid by shipping in the use of the sea marks provided, such as lighthouses and buoys.

Its office in Trinity Square, built by Samuel Wyatt in 1795, was burned out in the Second World War but by 1953 had been restored by the late Sir Albert E. Richardson. In the hall are preserved two old statues brought from the courtyard of the Trinity Almshouses. One, of a certain Captain Maples, dated 1683, sculpted by Jasper Latham, is the earliest-known statue in lead by an English sculptor.

Corn Exchange

It all started in a coffee house called the 'Baltic' whose owner, like Lloyd, put a room at the disposal of those merchants who laid their money out in imports, largely tallow, skins and hemp, from that northern area. Membership outgrew space and so the Corporation moved on to other accommodation, arriving in Mark Lane as early as 1747. Rebuilding came in 1828, and extension in 1852, after the repeal of the Corn Laws in 1845 brought massive imports of grain, making much more space necessary for the merchants, English and foreign, who were now dealing in it. Other trade was ousted and a brand new Corn Exchange was built in 1881.

This was completely destroyed in 1941 but has once again been rebuilt. Its glass roof extends from Mark Lane to Seething Lane, appropriately, because this was the place in medieval times where corn was threshed and winnowed, and that is the meaning of 'seething'. Today the Corn Exchange is the most important cereal market in Britain with about 525 firms in membership.

St Olave's, Hart Street

This has been summed up by one authority as 'a country church in the world of Mincing Lane', because it has kept its churchyard as a place of rest for the dead rather than developing it as a resting place for the living. Rebuilt in the fifteenth century on the thirteenth century crypt, it survived the Fire of 1666 but was terribly damaged in the Second World War, though that ancient crypt and the strong tower with its seventeenth-century brick upperworks withstood the onslaught. The church was rebuilt in 1954, incorporating the old memorials which survived as well as the seventeenth century pulpit and communion rails.

World-famous diarist Samuel Pepys (1633-1703) is buried here and so is his wife. Happily their monuments were saved and re-erected, for he called St Olave's 'our own church'.

The churchyard gateway bears on its pediment five skulls with other bones beneath them, a reminder of the Plague of 1665 and of its many victims said to be interred here. This is probably why Dickens gave the church the name of St Ghastly Grim in his *Uncommercial Traveller*.

Lloyd's

Nothing could be more modern, brash and bright than Lloyd's new offices in London House, towering above Fenchurch Street Station, but nevertheless this is the place to obtain information on that Edward Lloyd born around 1648 who started it all.

Marine insurance was introduced into Britain in the sixteenth century and London's increasing importance as a great centre of trade after the Civil War led to a demand for backers prepared to underwrite hazardous voyages in the name of commerce. Such men had set up in the Royal Exchange, but the Great Fire made them homeless, so they took over their favourite coffee house in Tower Street, run by Mr Edward Lloyd, moving with him to his new premises in Lombard Street in 1691, from which was published in 1696 for the first time *Lloyd's News, Printed for Edward Lloyd (Coffee Man)* . . .

Through the next century Lloyd's divided, expanded and diversified. The Registry of Shipping was founded in 1760. In 1769 the more business-like members of the group broke away to produce a *New Lloyd's List* at the New Lloyd's Coffee House in Pope's Head Alley. In 1774 they moved back into the Royal Exchange from which was issued that third edition of the Register of Shipping which made the term 'A1' a household word, meaning originally an 'A' class hull and 1st class equipment — a good insurance risk.

Lloyd's

Lloyd's List has been published since 1837 and is now *the* daily newspaper on the movement of shipping, freight, national and international industry.

The famous Lutine Bell, rung once when a total wreck is reported and twice when a ship is overdue, was recovered from the wreck of H.M.S. *Lutine*, lost on 9 October 1799 with an insured sum of some £200,000 on board. It was not until 1850 that salvage operations began. They lasted over nine years and recovered £25,000 in coin, the rudder, now made into a table, and that ship's bell.

In 1928, Lloyd's moved to its own building in Leadenhall Street, designed by Sir Edwin Cooper 'in a Latin mood', including the grand 'Room' which was the famous successor to the former cramped coffee house. That building has been abandoned, and Lloyd's continues in the premises planned by Terence Heysham and put up between 1952 and 1958 on the other side of Lime Street.

Edward Lloyd was not tempted into the world of underwriting, but remained a simple coffee-house keeper to the last. He has a simple memorial in St Mary's Woolnoth where he was a member of the vestry until his death in 1713.

Fenchurch Street Station

What an exciting and noisy novelty the steam train must have been to the horse-drawn City! The first railway station to be built there, in 1840, was Fenchurch Street. Today that station behind its white-painted, broad-arched pediment with the great clock in the centre looks positively antique against the over-shadowing bulk of smoked-glass-windowed, steel-framed London House — Lloyd's new home.

But that station façade of 1854, designed by George Berkely, Engineer to the London and Blackwall Railway, still stands up well to critical scrutiny. The Gothic look of its slightly later canopy, eleven little gables, all fretted, gives it a Swiss air in a City square — its forecourt where lunchtime sunshine brings out a small army of office workers to attack their lunch on seats beneath the trees. Meanwhile rail passengers hurry by to mount the broad stairway from street to platforms, with its cast-iron balustrades still showing off all the grandeur and importance of the railway in those first dramatic days of steam. The arches of the viaduct which brings the railway in have been taken over by the wine trade as a very suitable and convenient storage for wine.

All Hallows, Staining

Strolling down London Street from Fenchurch Street Station towards Mark Lane it is a surprise to see, among all the great blocks of new buildings, a lone tower standing in a paved yard beside Star Alley, completely railed off, with just one tombstone pushing up from the stony ground. While an iron gate gives access to the yard, the church tower door was firmly locked when we tried the handle. It was hard to envisage it as the tower of an active fifteenth century church when local parishioners crowded through that door to make their devotions. The main body of this church of All Hallows was demolished in 1870.

The raised paved platform which adjoins the tower covers a crypt chapel built originally into a bastion of the City wall near Cripplegate and transported here to be re-erected at the expense of the Clothworkers' Guild in 1872.

Staining is a curious name. Professor Eilert Ekwall, expert on City street names, connects it with the house or hostel where the people from Staines settled or stayed on visits to the ancient City, recorded as early as 1053.

St Margaret Pattens

In medieval times the eastern end of Eastcheap was the place to buy yourself a pair of pattens — those wooden platforms on iron rings of which the nearest modern equivalent is our 'overshoes' for wet weather and muddy by-ways. So it was that nearby St Margaret's, founded as far back as 1067, received its nickname. And if you wish to know what pattens looked like — this is where you may see them.

It is a thrilling place to wander about in because we know that Sir Christopher Wren was himself a regular worshipper here: his monogram 'CW 1686' is carved on the ceiling of a pew. This is one of a pair of canopied pews which are unique in City churches. He was the architect of this church during its rebuilding from 1684 to 1689. It was thoroughly restored in 1956, when the north gallery was closed in to provide 'conference rooms and a rest centre for clergy', for the church is now a Christian Study Centre.

The old, carved woodwork, dark against the white walls, the grey columns and the pretty eighteenth-century monuments contribute to this church's special atmosphere.

Leadenhall Market

Oh, the lovely smell of the seaside in the City of London! That is what greets the nose on turning in under the lofty portals of Leadenhall Market, where, under the glass-roofed arcade, the fishmongers, poulterers and butchers display their wares on slabs open to the street.

On this same spot the Romans built their Basilica and Forum — roughly equal to our town hall and law courts — around 100 A.D.; so, where lawyers strolled almost two thousand years ago, discussing law and order, we can follow in their footsteps, talking turkey, beef and haddock. The entrance to the arcade is really delightful. The pillars rise up to turret-like finials on each of which a golden pheasant proudly perches. The foundation stone is still clearly legible, showing that it was laid on 28 June 1881 by Henry Isaacs, Chairman of the Markets Committee of the Corporation of the City of London. Horace Jones was the architect who brought the fluted iron pillars and decorative panels into being and Mr Nightingale the builder put it all together from that foundation stone up to the dragons writhing across the Lime Street entrance, where they guard the City's arms.

We can imagine how the market must have impressed Victorian Londoners with its huge, splendid newness — such a contrast to the medieval network of stalls where Pepys, in 1663, bought a 'leg of beef, a good one, for sixpence'. Those ancient alleyways were preserved exactly in the ground plan for the modern market.

London Metal Exchange

'Like many of the financial institutions of the City of London, the LME developed to meet the demands of the industrial revolution in the last century which turned this country into the centre of the world's trade.' (City of London Guide).

Business is done in a furious few minutes of buying and selling which has to be seen to be believed, in a room in Whittington Avenue close by Leadenhall Market. Here men sit in a circle no more than twelve feet in diameter, facing each other on leather-padded benches. This constitutes the famous 'Ring' of international metal dealers who, in the process of buying and selling copper, tin, lead, zinc and silver, establish the official prices which obtain throughout the world. Although they may never see the thousands of tons of metal in which they deal daily, a complicated system of 'hedging' makes sure that all their agreements could be fully honoured at any given moment.

The exciting atmosphere of the Metal Exchange can only be appreciated by a personal visit, which can be arranged through the Secretary.

St Peter-upon-Cornhill

From the corner of Gracechurch Street and Cornhill, St Peter's looks shabbily unprepossessing, though the notice on the door proudly points out that it is the church of the Royal Tank Regiment and is 'reputedly the oldest church site in the City' having been consecrated in 179 A.D. and built upon by Lucius, 'the first Christian King of this land, then called Britaine' as a tablet in the vestry explains. But much of St Peter's today is unashamedly Victorian, including the painting and the windows at the east end.

The original work of Sir Christopher Wren over four years from 1677 is detectable in the shape of the church where square columns are used to form the nave and the aisles. The carved, wooden choir screen is said to be one of only two designed by Wren now in existence, though one authority gives the credit to Wren's daughter. There is much rich woodwork to be admired when the church is open, but even when it is not there is still the paved churchyard to be enjoyed, approached from Gracechurch Street and a path where wrought-iron gates surmounted by a lantern which shines on a gilded, rather chubby St Peter, complete with keys, give on to the churchyard where two great plane trees shade huge bowls of flowers. A quiet place where one can get a glimpse of the greened copper dome above which a spirelet carries, as a weathervane, the golden key of St Peter.

St Michael's Alley

'The narrow courts and passages off Cornhill have much to offer the City explorer,' says Geoffrey Fletcher, the celebrated artist. St Michael's is one of them, the place in London where coffee was first made as a beverage and sold, in 1657, by Pasqua Rosee whose coffee house stood on the site of the Jamaica Wine House.

In neighbouring Castle Court is the George and Vulture, rated by the same artist as 'the finest of the City's hostelries', where Pickwick admirers can drink the port for which it is famous while remembering that Dickens put Mr Pickwick in a room here to await the hearing of the breach of promise action taken against him by Mrs Bardell.

Lombard Street

Enter Lombard Street from Gracechurch Street and on the left one has the pleasure of seeing two charming pieces of what planners would call 'street furniture', pieces which are now part of our modern history. The blue-painted cast-iron police telephone box, for emergency use by the public, matches the tall litter bin with its semi-circular top sliding open like an old bread bin, with a clever little door in the side through which the containers themselves can be removed for emptying.

The street is admirably summed up by Arthur Mee, writing before the Second World War: 'It is a grim but dignified thoroughfare of banks and financial houses, and it is noted for the fine modern signs on many of the buildings. The Black Boy, the Cat and Fiddle, and the Jerusalem Artichoke all add a touch of levity to this solemn street.' But Mee's theory that it was named after the merchants and financiers from Lombardy, who replaced the Jews as money-lenders in the City, is rendered doubtful by Professor Eilert Ekwall who has traced it, as 'Langburnestrate', back to a will of 1285, with 'Lombardstrete' creeping in from 1318. His investigations suggest that, from the long tables set out as market stalls at one end of the street, it became 'Long-board-street' and by careless repetition, Lombard Street.

St Edmund, the King and Martyr

Whilst other churches speak, in their guides, of trial by fire in 1666 and 1940, St Edmund's in Lombard Street shows in a glass case the fragments of a bomb dropped by an enemy aircraft at 10 a.m. on 7 July 1917. It broke the main beam of the roof, which fell in, causing much damage to a building by Sir Christopher Wren, completed in 1679 with a steeple added by 1708.

Repairs were put in hand and the church was opened again on 1 October 1919. Now we can sit in peaceful contemplation of the highly decorated reredos, the woodwork beautifully carved against a gilt background which surrounds panels displaying in gilt on red the Lord's Prayer, the Commandments and the Creed. Its font takes us back to the seventeenth century and Wren's elegance, with a cover of the blackest wood crowned with figures of the four apostles and suspended by a curious bracket and chain. A memorial to Charles Melville Hays, President of the Grand Trunk Pacific Railway who was lost in the Titanic on 15 April 1912 brings us into the twentieth century again.

It is interesting to discover that Joseph Addison, the English essayist (1672-1719) walked down the aisle here with his bride, the Dowager Countess of Warwick, in 1716.

Mansion House

As the White House is to the President of the United States, so the Mansion House is to the Lord Mayor of London. The difference is in the age of the office — the citizens of London persuaded Prince John that they should have a representative in his government as early as 1191, but the present House for that man was not built until 1753, to the design of George Dance the Elder, 'Clerk to the City's Works' who began the undertaking by laying the foundation stone in 1739. The first mayor to take proud possession was Sir Crisp Gascoigne. He would have stood, as hundreds of his successors have, between the pillars of its portico to see processions pass and take the salute beneath a grand pediment which carries a tableau of the city in allegory with figures representing London and the Thames, Liberty, Commerce, and Plenty. The principal ceremonial rooms including the 'Egyptian Hall' can be seen by the public from Tuesday to Thursday upon written application.

In the ballroom the panels are decorated with groups of musical instruments except for one which unashamedly shows a representation of Leda and the Swan, an unusual subject for such a room. It could have been designed by Dance simply as a *trompe l'oeil* to astound the Lord Mayor's guests.

St Stephen, Walbrook

Some people say that St Stephen's pretty, greened copper dome, which still provides a view amongst the soaring office blocks behind the Mansion House, was put up by Sir Christopher Wren as a trial model for the great work of his life — St Paul's Cathedral. This was the famous architect's own parish, so no wonder that he put his heart into the work of rebuilding its church. His architect colleague, Sir John Vanbrugh (1664-1726) is buried here. He would have appreciated the finer points of the way in which Wren achieved a marvellous spaciousness in the relatively small rectangle beneath that lovely dome. Near the vestry door, pictures of this dome and that of St Paul's allow visitors to make an interesting comparison. The sixteen Corinthian columns which break up the rectangle of space are best seen from the north-west corner.

The very altar rails at which Sir Christopher Wren would have knelt, the font and its cover which he saw installed and the altar-piece on which he read the texts when the gilt letters were still drying have all, thankfully, been preserved to our sight. Who could believe, in looking round today, that St Stephen's was very badly damaged in the Second World War? The restoration in 1954, including glass by Keith New, is of a very high order.

St Mary Abchurch

Its interior is said by John Betjeman to be one of the most beautiful in the City. It also qualifies for inclusion in this book on historical grounds for it was put up three hundred years ago, in brick dressed with stone, to the designs of no less an expert than Sir Christopher Wren.

It did not escape damage in the Second World War, but this is not visible when one looks round the church today. The amazing painted dome is attributed alternatively to Sir James Thornhill, who painted St Paul's (by Godfrey Thompson), and to local painter-stainer William Snow in 1708 (by John Betjeman). Its restoration by Hoyle from 1948 to 1953, after bombing in September 1940, is of the highest sensitivity, matching the excellence of the complete refurbishment under the supervision of architect Godfrey Allen.

The splendid altarpiece shows carving by Grinling Gibbons and a similar standard of beauty is evident in the finishing of the pulpit and its sounding board, the font cover and the door frame. The eighteenth-century monuments and the ceremonial sword rests are fascinating accompaniments. The name 'Abchurch' derives from 'Up-church', simply indicating its position on a hill.

Temple of Mithras

In 1954, during the building of the huge new block of Bucklersbury House (completed 1958) on the triangle enclosed by Queen Victoria Street, Cannon Street and Walbrook, there were found the remains of a Roman temple built for the worship of the Persian god Mithras. A well associated with the temple, with its timber lining still intact, had to be filled in, but the stones of the temple were removed and re-assembled in the forecourt of Temple House immediately next to the pavement. The notice on the guard rail, at convenient leaning height, tells all: '. . . the Temple is seen as it appeared when uncovered some eighteen feet below the present level of Walbrook and on the bank of the original Walbrook stream.

'The Temple was built during the Roman occupation of London towards the end of the second century A.D. as a place of worship for the religious cult of Mithraism which was popular in the Roman army at this time.' Some of the objects found on the site have been preserved on display at Bucklersbury House and others have found a place in the Museum of London.

Poultry

The street that runs west from the Mansion House was originally that part of the 'cheap', or network of alleys making up the whole market area, where poultry was sold. It is written as 'Poletria' in a document dated as early as 1299 in the Letter Books of the City of London, meaning 'a place where fowls are sold for food'.

The building which dominates the street today is the headquarters of the Midland Bank, designed by Sir Edwin Lutyens, Gotch and Saunders and built between 1925 and 1928.

It is said that birds sold in Poultry were sent over to Scalding Alley where they were scalded in the Scalding House situated there to loosen the feathers for easier plucking in preparing them for the table.

Cheapside was always a main thoroughfare as well as the great market place of London. It was early known as Cheap or Westcheap and recorded as such very early in the twelfth century.

Mercers' Hall

This headquarters of a leading City livery company is now part of Becket House, on the corner of Ironmonger Lane and Cheapside. It was put up in 1958 in place of the former Hall, badly damaged in the Second World War, which itself stood on the site of that Hospital of St Thomas à Becket where the Mercers first came together as a guild and were incorporated in 1393.

Their name, in French, implied simply that they were merchants; they dealt at first in small goods, mainly wool and cloth, but eventually they came to control the trade in luxury cloths such as silk, velvet, cloth of gold and the like. Dick Whittington (died 1423) was a distinguished member; when Richard II was deposed in 1399 he still owed Dick a thousand marks for materials he had supplied for the King's Great Wardrobe.

The Mercers' Company is one of the richest City companies and is first in the order of precedence. There are still two reminders of the glory of the Mercers' former Hall. One is the Grinling Gibbons carvings which formed part of its sumptuous decoration and the other is their collection of plate which on ceremonial occasions is a wonder to see.

Bow Church

More properly known as St Mary-le-Bow, it derives its name from the church built on the site long before the Great Fire. It was then known as 'St Marie de Arcubus' because it was built on arches or 'bows' of stone. The Curfew Bell in its Norman tower marked the end of the apprentices' day at nine o'clock and from it the other City churches took their cue to join in the jangling chorus forever enshrined in our nursery rhyme of 'Oranges and Lemons'.

Wren's fine rebuilding after the Great Fire was begun in 1670, and crowned with the beautiful steeple rising some 220 feet from the ground, housing the famous peal of bells within whose sound a true Cockney is said to be born. It was the ancestors of these bells which are supposed to have rung out the thrilling inspiration, 'Turn again, Whittington, thrice Lord Mayor of London'.

Post-war repair of extensive war-time damage has been to the designs of Laurence King, who has kept the exterior as Wren planned it but has remodelled the interior to suit modern ideas on worship in, and use of, the church. The crypt, built at the end of the eleventh century, is said to be the oldest existing church structure in London. It has been used for meetings of the Ancient Court of Arches — the ecclesiastical court of appeal for the province of Canterbury.

Ye Olde Watling

Ye Olde Watling represents in this book all those scores of interesting places in the City where one can eat and drink and take one's ease. Partly destroyed in the Great Fire, the old house was rebuilt in 1668 and restored at least twice in the twentieth century, when care was taken to preserve its original architectural features. An old licence preserved on view lays down that every customer must order a proper meal before being served with liquid refreshment!

Its name comes from the Street in which it is situated and Watling Street would appear to get its name from the Vitellina Strata of the Romans — but this is a fallacy. It has no connection at all with the great Watling Street from Dover through London to Wroxeter. It was actually called 'Athelingstrate' in the thirteenth century — a reference to the land hereabouts belonging to an 'atheling' or prince of the royal blood. The confusion of the two names in the minds of medieval folk is perfectly understandable when we consider how few people then could read or write.

Panyer Alley Steps

'WHEN YE HAVE SOUGHT
THE CITTY ROUND
YET STILL THIS IS
THE HIGHEST GROUND
AUGUST THE 27
1688'

This verse can still be read on its original stone tablet, crowned by a bas-relief of a boy sitting on the kind of pannier in common use in those days for transporting goods or personal luggage. But the stone is not quite in its original position. Panyer Alley was an ancient lane, named from the pannier — or basket — makers who gathered here to make and sell their wares. It has been replaced in modern development leading to St Paul's Shopping Centre by Panyer Alley Steps which rise from Newgate Street.

Through the concrete-pillared passages where trees and seats break the hard and angular outline of the soaring office blocks there is the wide and breezy courtyard of Paternoster Square with views of St Paul's. The religious connection between the two is remembered in the sculpture 'Paternoster', by Elizabeth Frink, of a shepherd with his sheep, commissioned by Paternoster Development Ltd. and unveiled by Yehudi Menuhin on 30 July 1975.

St Paul's Churchyard

The preaching from the pulpit of St Paul's Cross in this yard was a very important feature of medieval life. The cross was first put up in 1191, destroyed by the earthquake of 1382, re-erected in 1449 and totally demolished in 1643 by order of the Long Parliament. The column we see in its place was the inspiration of H. C. Richards, who died in 1905 and provided for it in his will, 'to recall and to renew the ancient memories'. It was designed by Sir Reginald Blomfield and erected in 1910. The base is formed like the original pulpit but performed the function of a drinking fountain. Now it is green with age and no longer works, though the little cherub from whose lips the water once flowed looks serenely unconcerned.

On the other side of the Cathedral, a stark modern sculpture by Bainbridge Copnal representing 'Becket' was acquired by the City in 1973.

St Paul's Churchyard

Imagine the scene on the night of the Great Fire when the booksellers came scurrying from the bookshops in the alleyways all about the churchyard, bringing their books in armfuls and barrow loads to the Cathedral in which they thought these means of their livelihood would be safe under divine protection. They were not; it was just another incident in the long drama of this hallowed ground with its back-drop, black and grey, the walls of old St Paul's.

The railings are splendid in their vast proportions, with massive rounded spear-like tops, all of cast-iron made at Lamberhurst in Sussex in 1714. They have been carefully restored to enclose the enlarged space formed by the closure of the eastern side of St Paul's churchyard in 1966 to include it in the open space, made in 1878, of the ancient burial grounds of St Gregory by St Paul's and St Faith the Virgin under St Paul's.

In 1940 German bombs destroyed 'The Bible and Sun, No. 65, in St Paul's Churchyard' so there is now only a plaque on the wall of a big new building to remind us that John Newbery, the remarkable publisher and bookseller who lived from 1713 to 1767, had his publishing house and home here. He produced one of the first series of books specifically for children, including *Goody Two Shoes* and *Mother Goose*.

St Paul's Cathedral

The mother church of Britain and the Commonwealth has to be a show place, but if one takes a seat in a pew to gaze about, the noise of visitors speaking in every language under the sun becomes subdued. The wonderful sight within the cathedral engages the eye and the imagination to the exclusion of that bustle which begins at the bookstall, under the shredded banners of the Coldstream Guards hanging by the memorial to the Battle of Inkerman, 1854.

From one's pew, the view of the massive, square pillars under highly effective lighting is strangely intimate, beautiful and harmonious. To the uninformed sightseer the highly decorated choir has an eastern appearance with its unusual glittering mosaic scenes by Sir William Richmond (1843-1921), representing the Creation on the one hand and Christ in Majesty on the other. Above them in the spandrels of the great Dome other mosaics by artists such as G. F.

Watts and W. E. F. Britten portray the prophets and the evangelists. Above them people walking round the Whispering Gallery are reduced to the size of dolls while, even higher, marble statues of the Fathers of the Church look out from recesses all around beneath the cupola, 218 feet above the floor, where Sir James Thornhill painted in monochrome eight scenes from the life of St Paul.

St Paul's Cathedral

The crypt of St Paul's (entrance in the south transept) is a place of people. Their bodies have turned to dust but surely their spirits haunt this place, and what an august company they are. In Painters' Corner are Turner (died 1851), Landseer (died 1873), Millais (died 1896), Constable (died 1837) and many others.

St Faith's chapel at the east end contains seven monuments which to a greater or lesser degree escaped the Fire. On the farther side is Musicians' Corner and then there are the graves of great fighting men, such as Beatty, Jellicoe, Keyes and Roberts.

In a position below the very centre of the dome stands the huge sarcophagus of the Duke of Wellington made of porphyry (volcanic purplish-red rock). At the west end is his massive funeral car, made at Woolwich Arsenal from guns captured during his campaigns and weighing eighteen tons. At his funeral the car broke through the road surface and held up proceedings for an hour until it was pulled out again.

St Paul's Cathedral

To look at the monuments in the aisles and transepts is to turn the pages of British history with patriotic pride. Yet until 1795 no-one was commemorated in the Cathedral; now it is 'second only to Westminster Abbey in the number of its monuments to the mighty dead'.

The first monument to be admitted was the statue of

John Howard, 1726-90, the prison reformer, which stands on the right-hand side of the entrance to the south choir aisle; the second that of Dr Samuel Johnson, seen surprisingly in a Roman toga, on the opposite side, both sculpted by John Bacon the Elder. In 1796 Flaxman's statue of Sir Joshua Reynolds was put at the corner of the north transept, and from then on a flow began of which the most important include Nelson's monument in the South Transept, also by Flaxman, with figures like the naval officer holding a sextant which represent the North Sea, the Baltic, the Nile and the Mediterranean and Sir John Moore's against the wall of the South Transept, designed by John Bacon the Younger, a sad tableau of that brave man's death at Corunna in 1809. Lord Collingwood, General Gordon, Earl Kitchener and Lord Leighton are also represented.

The monument between the pillars of the north aisle to the Duke of Wellington (1769-1852) by Alfred Stevens is so tall and so busy with groups representing Truth plucking out the tongue of Falsehood and Valour putting down Cowardice that the man himself, mounted on his horse, is almost out of sight. He was not put there until 1912 when John Tweed, using Stevens' original designs, completed a work which was begun in 1856 but was still not finished when Stevens died in 1875.

Against the wall of the South Choir the figure of John Donne in a shroud sculpted by Nicholas Stone (1586-1647) is delicately, sombrely impressive. Donne, the famous poet and Dean of St Paul's died in 1631 and this is the only monument from the earlier St Paul's to have survived the terrible Fire practically intact.

St Martin-within-Ludgate

The old church of St Martin, rebuilt in 1437, stood just within the Roman wall near the Lud Gate which gives the present street its name. This little gate was the first curfew gate in London to be closed at night. 'Lud' probably means, 'the gate where one has to bow one's head to go in'.

The church we see today, dedicated to the soldier-saint Martin of Tours is appropriately the chapel of the Middlesex Yeomanry and of the Honourable Society of Knights of the Round Table. It was rebuilt by Sir Christopher Wren over ten years from 1677 with a slender spire specifically designed to act as a foil to the swelling dome of St Paul's. There is a fine original reredos with the Lord's Prayer, the Creed and the Commandments written in gilt on oak and in the carving of the door frames can be seen the open pea-pod which is said to be the 'signature' of Grinling Gibbons. The organ, dated 1684, is one of the famous 'Father Smith' organs made by Bernard Smith (1630-1708) and music is today an important part of the life of the church, with regular and frequent series of recitals employing many instruments and kinds of composition. The font, contemporary with the organ, has one of those fascinating palindromes in Greek inscribed around it which can be translated, 'Wash my sin, not my face only.'

Stationers' Hall

The Stationers derive their name from the Latin 'stationarius', the term used for those who lent books for copying by scribes and for study at university back in the fourteenth century, but it also embraced those who copied, bound and sold books in permanent shops rather than from the pitches of itinerant traders. The Guild of Stationers, formed in 1403, took in the printers when they began their new craft from 1476 and by 1557 it was elevated by royal charter to livery company status.

The post-Fire Hall was built by 1673, but it has thrice been renovated. Its exterior shows a refronting of 1800 to designs of Robert Mylne. His ceiling was brought crashing down in the Second World War, but has been replaced by reference to the original design. The stained glass windows represent William Caxton, the first English printer, William Shakespeare, William Tyndale, the martyred Bible translator, Thomas Cranmer, Archbishop of Canterbury and St Cecilia, the patron saint of music, whose feast was long held here. The large window given by Master Joshua Butterworth depicts Caxton showing a proof from his press to Edward IV and his queen Elizabeth.

It was as late as 1933 that the old Stationers and the new Newspaper Makers joined together in the Worshipful Company of Stationers and Newspaper Makers.

Amen Court

The roar of traffic down Warwick Lane between Ludgate Hill
and Newgate Street is muted where Amen Corner, off Ave
Maria Lane, gives way to a narrow private street of houses in
warm red brick. They line one side of the 'U' shaped court in
perfect harmony, with beautiful lanterns hanging over their
doorways like a motif in a pattern. They were built in the period
of and possibly to the design of Sir Christopher Wren, for the
use of the Canons Residentiary of St Paul's. Behind the bar
which excludes traffic, the sight of tricycles and scooters shows
that happy families of those same Canons continue to live here at
Amen Court.

The name links with other streets walked by the monks of old
in their procession to the Cathedral on Corpus Christi Day.
They began intoning the Lord's Prayer, in its Latin form, at
Paternoster Row, said 'Amen' to it at *Amen* Corner, chanted their
'Hail, Mary!' down *Ave Maria* Lane then crossed Ludgate Hill
into *Creed* Lane reciting the Creed.

Dotted about the court are flowers in big containers which on
inspection prove to be the leaden cisterns once used in the
houses. They are decorated, initialled and dated 1669, 1730 and
1750.

Cutlers' Hall

Thirty-three men and boys hard at work in all the processes required before a lump of metal becomes a fine, keen knife — that is the sight one can see in Warwick Lane, on the frieze which decorates Cutlers' Hall. It was carried out in terracotta in such deep relief and so realistically, that each figure has a positive character glowing in its features.

Strangely, since the work was not carried out until around 1885, guide books are divided in attributing the craftsmanship to Benjamin Crestwick and George Tinworth. The Beadle who answered our ring at the door declared in favour of the former and claimed it is the only such frieze by that artist now extant. He pointed out that the elegant ornamental door knockers in the form of elephants' heads represent the ivory from which the handles of all those knives were made. The standard of workmanship exacted by the Company from its members is brought out in the motto which can be translated, 'To succeed in good faith'. That good faith has certainly been kept by the company with the medical profession in the production of a range of superb medical instruments.

Newgate Street

From Warwick Lane the great bulk of the General Post Office building can be seen rearing up on the other side of Newgate Street. Its age is indicated by 'ER VII' prominent on its façade. Two plaques remind us that far back in the thirteenth century the Greyfriars established their monastery here, dissolved in 1538. By 1552 Christ's Hospital had taken its place; not so much a hospital in the modern sense as a home and school for poor children and a source of financial help for unfortunate adults. It became the famous 'Blue Coat School' which continued until 1902 when it was removed to a site in the country near Horsham. That was when the Post Office took over with a group of buildings that stretch across to King Edward Street, where the bronze statue on its granite plinth rising from the pavement reminds us that Sir Rowland Hill, who died in 1879, '. . . founded uniform penny postage' in 1840, an achievement which is hardly likely to be repeated.

Near it is the entrance to the National Postal Museum, opened in 1966, extended in 1969, formed from the marvellous collection presented to the nation by R. M. Philips and the unrivalled range of specimen stamps of the world acquired by the Post Office as a member of the Universal Postal Union from 1878 onwards.

Old Bailey

Though 'Old Bailey' is the name of the street connecting Newgate Street and Ludgate Hill, it always represented to me the fearsome glamour of the Central Criminal Court where I felt, with a child's innocence, that under the goddess with the scales so evenly suspended, justice was dispensed with scientific exactitude.

The bailey probably started out as a defensive work in front of the old city wall. Its criminal association began when the gallows was erected in medieval times just a stone's throw from the New Gate in the city wall. The gatehouse eventually became the place for holding the intended victims of the hangman's noose. It developed into the common jail for London and the County of Middlesex and court sessions at the Old Bailey sprang from the commission of Jail Delivery for Newgate. Thus the Central Criminal Court came into being. It sat in the old court house until 1907, when a new court was built to the design of E. W. Mountford, occupying most of the site of the old Newgate Prison, with this message on its pediment: 'Defend the children of the poor and punish the wrongdoer.'

In 1970 the extension designed by architects McMorran and Whitby was brought into use. Its façade exemplifies the best in modern building materials and techniques, with the added distinction that it successfully resisted a bomb set off by a terrorist in 1973. It fronts Old Bailey, from where there is access to its twelve courts while the six old courts are entered from Newgate Street.

Church of the Holy Sepulchre

From a seat in the churchyard, the Garden of Remembrance of the Royal Fusiliers, one can see, through the tops of the trees, Justice holding her sword and scales on top of the Old Bailey. The old handbell rung outside the condemned cell on the eve of execution is on show in the church, which is the largest in the City. It began as a rebuilding in 1450 on the site of an earlier Saxon church. The walls, the tower and the porch survived the Great Fire; the interior was rebuilt 'in the style of Sir Christopher Wren'.

Many interesting people are connected with this church: Vicar John Rogers, first Protestant martyr burnt at the stake in Smithfield (1555); Queen Elizabeth's tutor, Roger Ascham, buried here in 1568; William Harvey, astute propounder of circulation of the blood, married here in 1605; Sir Henry Wood, that much-celebrated founder of the 'Proms', sometime Deputy Organist, who died in 1944 and whose ashes are deposited in the Musicians' Chapel here under a simple laurel-wreathed stone. An inscription on the window dedicated to him states: 'He opened the door to a new world of sense and feeling to millions of his fellows.' Dame Nellie Melba is remembered in the same way.

Holborn Viaduct

Stand on the bridge and watch the river flowing beneath you. It is an ever-moving stream of traffic up and down Farringdon Street. This is surely one of the earliest fly-over road junctions. It was planned by William Haywood to bypass the very dangerous incline of Holborn Hill where it ran down to the vale of the old Hole Bourne. He designed a viaduct fourteen hundred feet long and eighty feet wide, including a great iron bridge, to cross the valley, demolishing no less than four thousand houses in the process! That was in 1867-9 and today's drivers are still appreciating it. The bridge is decorated with elegant figures of muses representing Fine Art and Science on one side and Agriculture and Commerce on the other. Winged lions, sculpted by Farmer and Brindley and cast by Elkington and Co. crouch on both sides, at each end. The pretty lamps on cast-iron columns have been rendered obsolete by today's standards of street lighting, but the old sign on the wall still usefully indicates the 'public staircase leading to Farringdon Street'.

The City Temple

This Nonconformist church actually dates back to about 1640. A century ago, when other churches were moving out to the growing suburbs, it was resolved to continue the ministry here and, as an introductory leaflet explains, 'Rebuilding was necessary and the bold decision was made to build under the new name — the City Temple (i.e. the Temple of the Lord in the City) — on the newly created Holborn Viaduct. The original church was opened in 1874.'

With the Second World War came almost total destruction in 1941. But faith triumphed over man's inhumanity, and the rebuilt City Temple was opened for worship again in August 1958. It was designed by Lord Mottistone and Paul Paget, who cleverly included the façade of the former church, to seat 1,400, with a theatre beneath the main hall to accommodate 800 people.

Its first minister in the days of its foundation was Dr Thomas Goodwin, Chaplain to Oliver Cromwell and distinguished scholar. From 1936 to 1960 the great preacher Dr Leslie Weatherhead drew capacity congregations. His bust, by K. Wojnavowski, is placed in the foyer.

St Andrew's, Holborn

Sir Christopher Wren was commissioned to repair St Andrew's not because it was ravaged by the Great Fire, but because it was falling down from sheer neglect. He had all of it demolished except for the tower, and that had to be re-faced. The church claims a history as far back as King Edgar, who ruled in the tenth century, and it has associations with more than one great name.

John Webster, the dramatist, who died around 1625, is buried here; William Hazlitt, the essayist, married Sarah Stoddart here in 1808. Benjamin Disraeli, son of a Jew, baptised here when twelve years old in 1817, became first a novelist, then Prime Minister. None of them could have foreseen the dreadful bombing of the Second World War which left the church a forlorn hulk. Yet still the interior of that medieval tower survived and all the rest was sympathetically restored between 1960 and 1962, including the tomb of Captain Thomas Coram, born about 1668 who, as the *Treasury of Biography* (1866) says: 'After great sacrifices and persevering exertions for years, he established and obtained a charter for the Foundling Hospital which ... so impaired his fortune that in his old age it became necessary to relieve his necessities by a public subscription.'

Holborn Circus

After the construction of the new Holborn Viaduct it was necessary to reconstruct the approach roads and so, in 1872, the Circus was designed anew. The central statue of Prince Albert was added in 1874. It has not won approval in the guide books, being described as 'inferior', 'a poor equestrian statue', and, 'with his cocked hat lifted in unmilitary fashion'. In the mêlée of modern traffic surging around him, the Prince appears to maintain total indifference.

The nineteenth-century buildings had a pleasing architectural unity which speculation, development and war have destroyed. There is the consolation that a new light is thrown on St Andrew's, the largest of Wren's parish churches in the City. It stands now in marked contrast with the soaring block of the *Daily Mirror* on the other side of the Circus, built in 1961 to the design of architects Anderson, Foster and Wilcox, rising 169 feet from the pavement and noted for the clever use of colour. It is the largest newspaper building in Britain.

Staple Inn

Who is right? One authority says Samuel Johnson wrote *Rasselas* in his Gough Street house; another says he wrote it here in 1759 in this 'unique and beautiful relic of Tudor London' to pay the cost of his mother's funeral. In *Edwin Drood,* Dickens set the house of Mr Grewgious in the 'little nook composed of two irregular quadrangles called Staple Inn'.

The 'staple' refers to the ancient wool market held on the site, the 'inn' was an Inn of Chancery, a kind of college of the legal university of the day. The black and white timbered façade was exposed in restoration work after it was purchased by the Prudential Assurance Company in 1884. At the time of its building, in 1586, those timbers were hidden beneath a protective coat of plaster. It was very badly damaged in 1944 when a flying bomb demolished the hall in one of the quadrangles, but it was restored again by 1950, using as much of the original material as possible, and it is now the headquarters of the Institute of Actuaries.

Smithfield

'The greatest wholesale meat market in the world' — that is one writer's judgment, and it certainly is the impression it gives at the peak of its early morning activity. From across the wide approach of West Smithfield the market buildings in red brick, white stone and blue ironwork with the entrance topped by the City arms supported by the familiar writhing dragons, look cheerfully modern. They date, though, from 1867 when the west wing was completed, followed a year later by the east wing, all at a cost in land and materials of £2 million. Down the central aisle, great iron gates beneath a huge, green four-sided clock give access to those wings where a veritable forest of large iron hooks display the meat for sale over some ten acres of floor space, including extensions up to the end of the century.

In 1174 Thomas à Becket's clerk described it as, 'A smooth field where every Friday there is a celebrated rendezvous of fine horses to be sold . . . ' In 1305 oxen were being sold for 5s 6d each; by 1533 prices were controlled: the maximum price of beef being one halfpenny a pound. Today the London Central Market, better known simply as Smithfield, has its own police force, its own public house open from 6.30 a.m. and cold stores which hold several thousand tons of meat.

Smithfield

From 1150 the 'smooth field' on the edge of the City was the main fair ground for the sale of horses and cattle. Until the reign of Henry IV it was also the place of execution, being used for this purpose because it was such a public gathering place. A monument against the wall of St Bartholomew's Hospital, erected at the expense of the Protestant Alliance, remembers '. . . martyrs of religious persecution who were burned 1555-7, John Rogers, John Bradford, John Philpot and others.'

The gibbet also stood in the field and criminals dangled from it as a salutory example in an appropriate place, for the fair, sometimes called Bartholomew Fair, including the Cloth Fair which now names a street, had descended by Elizabethan times into a noisy, brawling fun fair, renowned for the kind of behaviour which even in 1815, when it was in decline, produced forty-five cases of lawbreaking in one day. By 1855 the fair had disappeared and Smithfield was a far cry from those days of knightly splendour when Edward III ordered a seven-day tournament to be held there in 1374. Here it was, too, that, in 1381, the rebel leader Wat Tyler, at the head of a great mob, confronted King Richard II and met his match; he was killed and the boy-King won over the hostile crowd.

St Bartholomew-the-Great

Down Cloth Fair, in an area looking sad under demolition and development, there stands the Church of St Bartholomew-the-Great, strong and secure in flint and stone, with the verger's house of brick and tile built straight onto the nave in a striking contrast which caused John Betjeman to describe it as, 'looking like a Cotman water colour and a reminder of the East Anglian quality of the City . . . '

It owes its foundation to Rahere, an English churchman of Frankish descent who, recovering from illness on a pilgrimage to Rome, vowed he would found a hospital in his own country. He secured the grant of the Smooth Field (Smithfield) by Henry I and in 1123 began the building of a Priory to which the hospital was attached. In it he installed the Augustinian Canons who looked to him as their Prior. The priory church was a grand edifice with a nave and choir 310 feet long, and a massive tower which was brought tumbling down by the 1382 earthquake.

There is another entrance to the church through the thirteenth century gateway in Little Britain. Above it was built, in Tudor times, a timber-framed house. Its age and structure was unsuspected until a bomb dropped by a Zeppelin in 1915 blew off some surface tiles and showed the timbers beneath. That gateway was the actual porch of the former church which stretched right down the churchyard to the present door. The whole structure was thoroughly restored in 1932 in memory of the brothers Webb, who had worked for forty years on the restoration of the church itself.

St Bartholomew-the-Great

At the suppression of the Priory the church was robbed of all its treasures and much of its building. Only the choir was left to serve as the parish church. In that choir the founder's tomb survived. Rahere died in 1144, but his tomb is of a fifteenth century re-making. Under a very beautiful canopy, on a tomb which still contains his remains, Rahere's effigy lies in his prior's habit, holding a Bible open at Isaiah 51:3, the text of which epitomizes Rahere's work in draining the Smooth Field and turning it into 'the garden of the Lord'. All around can still be seen the massive pillars of the original Norman building. The brick tower is a seventeenth-century construction, along with the wooden turret which houses the oldest complete ring of bells in London. But the five bells, dating from 1510, are not rung because the Hospital is so near at hand.

Around the church in the old monastic buildings, all sorts of industrial work developed. The present Lady Chapel was a printing office in which Benjamin Franklin worked for a year. It later became a fringe factory, supported on iron columns above what is now the High Altar. The north transept at that time was a blacksmith's shop. Even the crypt, once a charnel house, had been made into a wine and coal cellar. It says much for the devoted Rectors and parishioners that since the latter half of the nineteenth century, when the church was well restored, these workplaces have been bought back and brought again into religious use.

St Bartholomew's Hospital

From Giltspur Street round West Smithfield and down Little Britain stretches the parish of St Bartholomew the Less. In other words, St Bartholomew's Hospital. The block in Giltspur Street bears the legend 'School of Medicine 1878' across its soot-stained stone facade; in West Smithfield a pillared pediment frames an inscription which tells us that the hospital was founded by Rahere in 1102 and refounded by Henry VIII in 1546 and the present building 'erected 1842 — Architect Philip Hardwicke'.

The gatehouse entrance was built in 1702 and frames in a pillared niche above the archway a statue of Henry VIII in recognition of the fact that, having taken over the property of the Priory, he returned the hospital to the Citizens. The walls within the gatehouse are inscribed as a war memorial. Passing through it one is surprised to come upon a large paved courtyard, where, in the shade of tall plane trees, a fountain, erected in 1859, splashes into a wide bowl where huge goldfish cruise about in water so clear that one can see that the bottom is covered with coins. No doubt every coin represents a wish for the recovery of a patient in the wards ranged all around.

The Fat Boy

High on the wall of the corner-house where Cock Lane meets Giltspur Street can be seen a fat little boy with his arms crossed, all gilt and gleaming. This is near that Pye Corner which is popularly supposed to be the northernmost limit of the Great Fire of 1666. One Robert Hubert 'a poor lunatic Frenchman of Rouen' was tried, found guilty of setting light to London, and hanged for it, though it was shown that he was not even in the capital on the day. It has now been established, as far as it can ever be, that the Fire started accidentally at about 2-3 a.m. on Sunday 2 September 1666 in the house of a baker named Farryner in Pudding Lane.

One preacher later made the point that London was being punished by God for the sin of gluttony, because the fire began in Pudding Lane and ended at Pye Corner! That corner derives its name not from food but from the fact that the old court of 'pied poudre' or 'dusty feet' was held on this site to try cases arising from bad behaviour at the nearby fair. The Fat Boy, representing gluttony, was actually put up outside the old 'Fortune of War' tavern near its present location.

Penny Post

On the west side of King Edward Street outside the large cluster of buildings of the Post Office stands the statue of Sir Rowland Hill, who was born in 1795 and died in 1879. He early attracted attention as a schoolmaster (until 1833) with his own system of teaching self-discipline and as a founder-member of the Society for the Diffusion of Useful Knowledge. In 1837 he published his 'Post Office Reform,' suggesting a system of postage throughout Britain at a low and comprehensively applicable rate, using pre-paid stamps.

He can be said to be directly responsible for the 'Uniform Penny Postage' introduced on 10 January 1840. In 1846 he was made Secretary to the Postmaster General and in 1854 to the Post Office itself. He established book post in 1848 and reformed the money order and postal packet services. The importance of his work was recognized by a grant from Parliament when he retired and by his burial in Westminster Abbey.

Butchers' Hall

Its foundation is lost in history as the Hall of one of the seven oldest Livery Companies. Stow's *Survey* states that a Butchers' Hall stood in Farringdon Ward back in A.D. 975 and there are definite records from 1179. On 23 April 1377 the Butchers' Company, after complaints, were ordered not to sell best lambs for more than twelve pence. Others could go for eight to ten pence. This is the first known record of price control!

The Great Fire destroyed the Hall and impoverished the Company, which had been granted its arms in 1540 with a motto which can be translated, 'Thou hast put all things under his feet, all Sheep and Oxen' — a quotation from the eighth Psalm. It was finally granted a Charter of Incorporation in 1605. The Hall built after the Fire was compulsorily acquired for the development of the Metropolitan and District Railway in 1884, so the Company decided to take the opportunity of finding a site nearer Smithfield, the real home of their trade. Their Hall was built once again, in Bartholomew Close, and opened in 1885. In September 1915 it was severely damaged by bombs from a Zeppelin. It was repaired, only to be totally ruined by a flying bomb in July 1944. But those butchers are dogged people. In 1959 another foundation stone was laid and so the members of the Company meet today in another splendid Hall. A phoenix if ever there was one!

The Museum of London

The newest building with the oldest contents — the one place which *must* be visited if the City's history is to be appreciated. The collections of the Guild-hall Museum and the London Museum, founded in 1911 by Viscount Esher and Harcourt, have been brought together and most superbly arranged in the brand new building designed by Powell and Moya right next to the Barbican Centre. The Museum was opened on 1 June 1975, 'to show more fully than ever before how one square mile of the Roman city of Londinium developed into the modern Greater London conurbation of 610 square miles'.

There is 50,000 square feet of exhibition space arranged on two floors. The permanent collections are supplemented with changing exhibitions and a programme of events in the cinema-cum-lecture-theatre. It is impossible to describe in a few words the wonderful range of exhibits and the care with which they are shown in relation to each other — from the Lord Mayor's coach to the Centurion's tombstone. It certainly fulfils its aim 'to bring archaeology alive, showing the effect of war, plague, fire, fashion, business and now tourism on a city that is of local, national and international significance'.

London Wall

The Roman wall which gives the name to the present street is thought to have been built at the beginning of the second century A.D. Its course has been traced back via Bishopsgate and Aldgate to the Tower, and from the present London Wall forward to Aldersgate, Newgate and Ludgate to continue along the river bank back to the Tower again. Thus it extended three miles to enclose some 325 acres.

Until the middle of the eighteenth century the wall stood strong and tall all down the north side of the street, though the space before it was in two places occupied by the churchyards of All Hallows-on-the-Wall and St Alphage. For years pulling down the wall provided stone for building houses on it, in front of it and behind it. By 1800 a large section at the Finsbury Square end was demolished 'to allow more sunshine in the front of Bethlehem Hospital' to quote Sir Walter Besant (*London: City*, 1910).

At that time the street had a very different appearance of age and picturesqueness, with its two churches, Sion College and the Armourers' Hall against the background of that wide and ancient wall.

Barbican

The official guide to the City says that 'pedestrianization' will continue so that, 'by 1985 it will be possible to walk from Aldgate to the Law Courts without having to cross a main road . . . the Barbican is, of course, completely pedestrianized.' The Barbican scheme was designed to redevelop 63 acres of bombed-out ruins of the pre-war commercial district. A barbican in Roman times was a line of fortification including a watchtower, and the remains of just such a wall and fort have been traced through the area. Under County Council architect Sir Leslie Martin, the development began in 1962, continuing under his successor Sir Hubert Bennett, to provide a commercial complex and a separate site for residential blocks to house some 6,000 people supported by theatre, concert hall, library and 'local' together with all the necessities of modern life in London.

Not the least of them is a pleasing environment. From the south side of London Wall it is possible to walk above the rush of traffic straight into the balconies of the Barbican. From here there are delightful views of the extensive water features which give greenness to the gardens and which lap at the foot of the mighty remains of that Roman wall and bastion.

St Giles', Cripplegate

Right in the middle of the brand new Barbican development, surrounded by its wide-spreading yard of purply-red bricks and a further view of lakes and schools and flats there stands St Giles', a church built in 1390. How could its builders have guessed what vicissitudes it would overcome in the next six hundred years? In 1545 it was ravaged by fire, and over the next two centuries it had to be rebuilt and restored against the ravages of time itself. The tower, for example, shows upperworks of brick built by John Bridges in 1683. It was restored again in Victorian times as its external appearance shows. The inside, though, reminds us, in its modern restoration by Godfrey Allen, that it was bombed in the first German attack on the City on 24 August 1940 and burnt out in the second great fire of London on the night of 29 December of the same year. It was not until 1960 that its refurbishment was complete, and the east and west windows and the organ were renewed by 1969.

Personalities connected with St Giles' include Shakespeare, who came here for his nephew's baptism in 1604, Oliver Cromwell, who walked down the aisle with his bride in 1620 and John Milton, who was buried here in 1674.

St Alphage

Along the High Walk on the north side of London Wall everything looks new from the dual carriageway and the City Business Library on the one hand to the blocks of the Barbican on the other. So we are surprised to see the ancient remains which rise up to the walkway from the old pavement level. This pathetic ruin started out in the fourteenth century as the tower of the chapel of the Priory of Elsing Spital, founded in 1329 and devoted to the care of one hundred blind men.

It was incorporated into the second Church of St Alphage at the time of the Reformation. The original eleventh century church which was dedicated to that Alphage, Archbishop of Canterbury, who met his martyrdom at the hands of the Danes in 1012, lay a little further to the north against the old City wall. It was demolished, as a ruin, when this chapel of Elsing Spital was taken over as the parish church.

The remains we see of the chapel were lost to sight for hundreds of years in the jungle of buildings which grew over the area. They were only brought to light by the fierce bombing of 1940. The later church, built in 1777, was demolished and taken away in 1924.

Pewterers' Hall

Mentioned as an organized body in 1348, the Company's first charter is dated 1473, though a coat of arms was granted twenty-two years earlier. Until well into the eighteenth century, pewter, an alloy of tin and lead, or of tin and some other metal, was used for all kitchen utensils as well as for more decorative dining implements and also for works of art, so the Company had an important function in maintaining standards in the quality of the metal. As pewter was gradually superseded by pottery, glass and steel, the Company's influence declined, but even today it authorizes a special mark to be applied to the best quality pewter.

The present Hall, in neo-Georgian style, was built in 1961, just four hundred and sixty-five years after the first Hall was erected, but not on the same site. The second Hall, built after the Fire, was demolished in 1932 and its land in Queen Victoria Street exchanged for the present site in Oat Lane near St Paul's. The panelling and chandeliers from the former Hall have been preserved in the new building which was designed by David Evelyn Nye and Partners.

Haberdashers' Hall

Haberdashers have been plying their trade in small articles of costume accessory for so long that the origin of their name is quite unknown. In contrast their present Hall is almost as new as it could be, being built in 1956 as part of the office block called Garrard House, designed by Arthur S. Ash, on the corner of Gresham Street and Wood Street.

Their first Hall on the same site, fronting Staining Lane, was put up in 1448 when they received their first charter as 'the Fraternity of St Catherine the Virgin of Haberdashers of the City of London'. It lasted right through until the cataclysm of 1666. The second Hall was damaged by a fire in 1840, rebuilt in 1864 and completely demolished by a German air attack on 29 December 1940. The present Hall preserves several reminders of the long history of the Haberdashers, including the Company's records, paintings by Sir Joshua Reynolds and other famous artists, the figurehead of the impressive 'barge' the Company once sported on the Thames, and period furniture and clocks. The splendour of their Hall matches the record of those forty-one Haberdashers who have greeted the London populace from the inside of the Lord Mayor's coach.

Goldsmiths' Hall

'The Goldsmiths have been in the district (Aldersgate) for nearly six centuries, as the site occupied by their beautiful modern Hall has been the property of the Guild since 1340,' says R. J. Blackham in his *London Forever*. The Hall fronts Gresham Street between Gutter Lane and Foster Lane and the one we see today is a rebuilding to Philip Hardwick's Renaissance style designs in 1835.

As one would expect, this Livery Company has a remarkable collection of plate — 'their silver salts are their pride and glory,' writes Arthur Mee. Its hall-mark of a leopard's head is seen on so much gold and silver plate because it has had the responsibility for assaying and approving the quality of metal in gold and silver objects since the reign of Edward I. The charter of incorporation granted in 1327 demanded that, 'The wardens every quarter, once, or oftener, if need be, shall search in London, Southwark, and Westminster, that all goldsmiths there dwelling work true gold and silver . . . '

Representatives from the company have been summoned by the Lord Chancellor annually to form a jury to inspect freshly minted coins in the ceremonial 'Trial of the Pyx' — the name referring to the boxes in which the denominations of coins are delivered for testing.

St Mary Aldermanbury

It was not the church which drew our attention — it was the welcome sight of a seat in a little bower which promised rest and protection from the heat and noise of the traffic. We sat facing a remarkable memorial. Before we reached it, we had spotted Shakespeare's bust in bronze (by Charles J. Allen, 1805) standing out black against the green leaves. Now we sat and read a long inscription on a granite obelisk, not about him, but about his fellow actors John Heminge and Henry Condell ' . . . They lived many years in this parish and are buried here. To their disinterested affection the world owes all that it calls "Shakespeare"; they alone collected his dramatic writings regardless of pecuniary loss and, without hope of any profit, gave them to the world. They thus merited the gratitude of mankind.'

When we think how great the loss to literature would have been but for these two men we understand why Charles Clement Walker of Lilleshall Old Hall in Shropshire was happy to pay for the erection of this tribute in 1896.

Then it was that we realized the open space we were enjoying had been the churchyard of St Mary Aldermanbury, of which only the foundations remain in the close-cut turf because the ruins of this Wren church, bombed in 1940, were dismantled and taken across the Atlantic to be reassembled on the campus of Westminster College, Fulton in the United States, as a memorial to Sir Winston Churchill, who made his famous speech about the Iron Curtain at that College.

Guildhall

From the modern entrance one approaches the porch, fifteenth century survivor of fire and war, which in its vaulting shows the arms of Edward the Confessor and Edward VI with symbols of the four evangelists. Passing through it one is in the Great Hall where large windows of coloured glass shed muted light on monuments of heroic proportions in keeping with the character and deeds of the men remembered. Nelson's victories are listed on a monument where Britannia mourns his loss and naked Neptune looks on amazed. Beside it Sir Winston Churchill sits so simply in powerful isolation — in an armchair — while the Duke of Wellington (1796-1852) stands highest of all on a

pedestal inscribed 'Wisdom Duty Honour' flanked by two allegorical figures. William Pitt's inscription is nothing less than fulsome, supported with personification of his qualities, and animals and cherubs rollicking about in the prosperity he engendered. William Beckford, bent in obeisance, has his speech to George III of 23 May 1770 written out in full, because he had the courage to reprove the monarch publicly for his language concerning his Citizens of London.

The floor, said to be original, is especially pretty in grey, black and white; silver lead inlay in the stone representing shields and heraldic motifs.

Guildhall

The seventeenth-century Cockneys who saw the very symbol of their good government engulfed in the flames of the Great Fire could not have imagined a day when fire would rain from the sky to burn down their Guildhall once again. But such is the spirit of the City that rebuilding soon took place.

So Gog and Magog, lost in the Blitz, were recarved in lime wood and installed in their old place in 1952 through the generosity of Sir George Wilkinson, who was Lord Mayor over the period including that terrible night of 29 December 1940 when incendiary bombs destroyed the roof and most of the stained glass windows.

These two grotesque figures, weirdly out of proportion, are really of unknown origin. It is said that they represent the chiefs of the battling nations when Brute came all the way from Troy to push the boundary of his empire further west. Another version, quoted by Caxton, is that they were the last two survivors of a race of giants which inhabited the British Isles. Brute took them prisoner and set them to guard the gate of his London palace. They were first set up in the days of Henry V as wickerwork and pasteboard figures which were carried in procession at the Lord Mayor's Show. In 1708 they were replaced by the wooden effigies which perished in the Blitz.

Guildhall

Such a centre of administration in a great and busy city must be altered, extended and redesigned time and again as the requirements of government change. The Guildhall was first built between 1411 and 1426, so no doubt it was old and inadequate when the Great Fire of 1666 crackled through its rooms. It was rebuilt, though the porch itself survived. On its vaulted ceiling can be seen the arms of Edward the Confessor and Henry VI together with the symbols of the four Evangelists.

Through that porch, to their trials, came Anne Askew in 1546; Lady Jane Grey in 1554; Dr Garnett, the Jesuit accused of complicity in the Gunpowder Plot in 1606, and many others. The Great Hall in which they stood with sinking hearts was thoroughly restored in 1671 and again in 1870. The timber roof put up then was destroyed in the Blitz, and was replaced by 1954 with stone arches supporting a panelled ceiling. Nowadays the most dramatic event to take place here, amongst all the meetings for which it is used, is the Lord Mayor's annual banquet.

The present impressive façade was raised in 1789 to the design of George Dance, Junior. Over the porch the City Arms show fiery dragons supporting a shield bearing the cross of St George and the sword of St Paul, with the motto, *'Domine dirige nos'* — 'O Lord, guide us.'

Guildhall Library

Surely the best-known public library in the British Isles, certainly the oldest, founded in 1425 through the benevolence of Dick Whittington and William Bury, and without doubt one of the most comprehensive. The Guildhall Library preserves and makes available some 200,000 items in a collection which includes not only printed books but also manuscripts which ante-date the printing process, and maps and prints and other illustrations in their thousands. Its collection of books on the City of London is unrivalled, and the library of general works attracts students from all over the world.

The librarian receives and answers inquiries from many countries, particularly in the fields of English history, genealogy, heraldry and, of course, London in all its aspects. In the Whittington Room there is an ever-changing exhibition of books, manuscripts and prints from the Library's superb collection, which includes treasures such as the fourteenth century missal of St Botolph and one of only six examples now extant of Shakespeare's signature. The modern, very comfortably equipped Library can be used freely, for reference, by anyone, six days a week.

St Lawrence Jewry

It is something of a shock to enter into the cool and roomy interior of St Lawrence because it reflects the skill of modern craftsmanship in a manner which takes the breath away. It matches the artistry of Sir Christopher Wren's workmen who rebuilt the church after the Great Fire. The second rebuilding was necessary because the church was burnt out on the terrible night of fire of 29 December 1940 when the inferno created by incendiary bombs was altogether beyond the capacity of all the fire engines from miles around.

This unwished-for opportunity to demonstrate the continuing vitality of English craftsmanship was grasped with both hands. For example, the gloomy stained glass windows of Victorian introduction were lost: they were replaced by clear glass with some restrained coloured work on the lines of Wren's original intent, and Christopher Webb's dignified human figures join all the windows in one pleasing design. This is completed by the window in the vestibule which shows the original architect Wren, with Grinling Gibbons and Edward Strong, his Master Carver and Master Mason, above their modern counterparts, including architect Cecil Brown, who laboured for three years from 1954. There is no room here to enlarge upon the many points of interest but I can refer the reader to the informative and very cheap guides to glass, bells and organ, and a 'tourist's guide' available on the spot.

A farewell glance at the spire takes in the weathervane, incorporating with the original gridiron (reminder of St Lawrence's martyrdom by being roasted alive) an incendiary bomb, the cause of the destruction which brought the phoenix from the flames for the second time. We felt we could echo Samuel Pepys's remarks after the first rebuilding: 'Well pleased with the church, it being a very fine church.'

St Margaret Lothbury

Much as I would like to have given an interesting origin for 'Lothbury' even the expert I consulted could only comment, 'The name has been a good deal discussed.' But St Margaret's continues indifferent to the etymological curiosity of mere man while collecting within its walls the reminders of vanished City churches.

The elegant screen in dark, carved wood was brought here from All-Hallows-the-Great, a Wren church demolished in 1894. Through it one sees the altar-piece, carefully restored after World War Two by Rodney Tatchell, with beautiful, gilded recitals of the Ten Commandments, the Creed and the Lord's Prayer, and either side large paintings of Moses and Aaron which came from another church, St Christopher-le-Stocks, demolished in 1781.

The pulpit and sounding board, with its charming cherubs, display carving attributed to Grinling Gibbons. In the south aisle can be seen the altar-piece and some of the memorials from St Olave's which was levelled in 1888, though its tower was left and still stands in Ironmonger Lane. So, St Margaret's, built by Wren between 1686 and 1690, keeps green the memory of old churches where once a seething population of City dwellers crowded in to pray in faith and hope.

The Bank of England

Until 1 August 1973 the Bank of England was guarded every night by the military — a squad from the Brigade of Guards had protected it ever since the general alarm caused by the Gordon Riots in 1780.

The idea of such a bank was put forward by William Paterson (though he was not one of its founders) in 1694, under a Royal Charter which was renewed in 1946. Its original capital was £1,200,000 and its premises for the first forty years were in Grocers' Hall, by which time George Sampson had designed and built its own home. The present building was completed over fourteen years just prior to the 1939 War to the plans of Sir Herbert Baker, but the great blank outer wall rising from the street and supported by Corinthian columns is the single storey 'strong room' created by Sir John Soane, the Bank's official architect, around 1790. It is still mightily impressive from street level though seven modern stories soar above it.

The great pediment that crowns columns and figures carries a representation of Britannia with a model of the old Bank resting on her lap and flanked by a pile of coins. It is from this that the Bank derives its nickname the 'Old Lady of Threadneedle Street'.

A charming little feature of Soane's original building which has been preserved can be seen at the northwest corner at the end of Princes Street. It has been dubbed 'the Temple' by irreverent bankers because Soane based it on the Temple of the Sybil at Tivoli. When traffic demanded a widening of the road a new pavement was formed by cutting the corner below the 'temple' and supporting a domed passageway on nine pillars.

Threadneedle Street

Can you believe that one of the richest streets in the world got its name from a children's game? Professor Eilert Ekwall, in his *Street-Names of the City of London*, has advanced the idea that this broad street was, in medieval times, very suitable for the game of 'threadneedle' in which children form two rows facing each other, holding hands to make an arch, under which the front two run to join in the arch at the other end, gradually moving all down the street!

Another theory is that a trade sign showing three needles hung in the street at one time and so identified it for the illiterate and gave it the name. A third suggestion is that here was the home of the Needlemakers' Company whose coat of arms was a representation of three needles.

In 1765 a disastrous fire burned down some ninety houses in Cornhill and Threadneedle Street. The Bank of England, only thirty years or so old at the time, survived to become known affectionately the world over as 'The Old Lady of Threadneedle Street' and a modern personification of the 'Old Lady' can be seen on the pediment. (*See* Bank of England.)

Royal Exchange

'What's the golden grasshopper for, stuck up there on that pole?' many a tourist must have wondered when walking along Cornhill. The answer is that it crowns the 180 feet high clock tower of the Royal Exchange because it was the sign used as the seal of the Gresham family at least as early as the fifteenth century and it was Sir Thomas Gresham who founded the 'Bourse' as he called it, in 1568. Queen Elizabeth gave it her Royal Charter and the name Royal Exchange when she visited it in 1571.

Thomas Gresham was an astute financier who had noted the success of the Antwerp exchange and so copied it — a place where merchants could meet in 'walks' spaced round a quadrangle open to the air. His Royal Exchange was yet another casualty of the Great Fire of 1666 and its successor was burned down in 1838, so the present building dates only from 1844 when it was opened by Queen Victoria. Its architect, Sir William Tite, made sure that Gresham's part as founder should be remembered by putting his statue in a niche high up on the clock tower, which houses a peal of bells on which well-known airs are rung four times a day.

The Exchange ceased operating in 1939. It continues today as an exhibition hall. One can stroll round quite freely admiring the huge paintings which grace the walls. They tell the story of events in the history of the City from the Phoenicians trading with the Britons to William II building the Tower of London and so on through to the Great War, interspersed with portraits of people remembered and forgotten. All of them are seen in a dim, mysterious light, which hardly seems to reach the corners in which statues of Queen Victoria and her Consort, Queen Elizabeth and Charles II are placed almost apologetically.

Under the glass-domed roof is the original floor of that first exchange. Gresham walked here with his Queen, and we can follow in his footsteps — a strangely satisfying experience.

Royal Exchange

From the shadowy interior one looks out through vast pillars which frame the war memorial raised by public subscription to the men of London who served in the 1914-18 War, with a postscript embracing all those men and women who served in World War Two. It is a simple yet impressive obelisk designed by Sir Aston Webb with figures by Alfred Drury; soldiers standing solemnly remind us of those thousands who gave without counting the cost and did their duty without seeking any reward, so that we can still walk about our beloved London in freedom.

Thanks to them the age-old custom of ceremonially proclaiming a new sovereign from these steps continues. At the apex of the triangular forecourt there rises up on a brown stone plinth the bronze statue of the Duke of Wellington on horseback, riding, it will be seen, without stirrups! It was sculpted by Sir Francis Chantrey and put up in 1844, thus matching the newness of the third Royal Exchange. From the statue the pillared façade of the Exchange can be best appreciated. In the 'tympanum' or framed gable can be seen the deeply carved personification of 'commerce' holding that Royal Charter of 1571 and attended by a host of people led by the Lord Mayor with British merchants and foreigners in attendance.

Stock Exchange

It is surprising to learn that the London Stock Exchange deals in nine times the number of securities listed by the Wall Street exchange. Founded in 1801, the Stock Exchange is a large and vital cog in the machinery of Britain's economy, because by accommodating the buying and selling of securities it is instrumental in raising the capital needed for the expansion of industry and trade.

The Exchange developed from the business of the Royal Exchange (*q.v.*). Later the money dealers left it and set up business in Change Alley off Cornhill, using Jonathan's Coffee House for many of their stock-jobbing transactions. By the early eighteenth century, merchants were becoming speculative financiers, needing the help of stock-jobbers who, growing in importance, moved into their own headquarters in Threadneedle Street some time after 1750, calling it 'New Jonathan's' until 1773 when they decided to put up over the door the new title of 'The Stock Exchange'.

It was in 1801 that it was put on a new basis in a new building in Capel Court, but this and later buildings have all been overtaken by the recent building of the huge, skyscraper block in Old Broad Street.

St Andrew Undershaft

This ancient church was built between 1520 and 1532, but as we see it today it is the subject of much restoration, for the tower was rebuilt in 1830 and the chancel in 1875. Two memorials serve to show the length and range of life this church has served. One to the memory of Mrs Elizabeth Forsteen shows that a mother was missed then as sorely as she is today:

'Of manners mild, to all who knew her dear,
The tender mother, best of Friends lies here . . .
Dearest of Mothers! best of Friends! farewell!
May this plain stone a son's Affection tell . . .'

The other is a fine monument in black marble and alabaster to John Stow, restored to all its former glory in 1979 by students on the Stone Conservation Course at Croydon College under the supervision of John Green. Stow, who lived from 1525 to 1605, is shown seated at the writing desk, where he had penned such works as *Annals, or a General Chronicle of England* and the famous *Survey of London and Westminster,* published in 1598. The quill pen in his hand is renewed annually on the Sunday nearest 5 April, the date of his death, a touching little ceremony.

St Katharine Cree

Going west from Aldgate along Leadenhall Street, St Katharine's will be found on the right at the junction with Creechurch Street. Its 'Cree' is thought to be an elision of 'Christ Church', from the original foundation here of an Augustinian priory in the twelfth century. The present tower was built in 1504; the rest of the church in 1631, in a Renaissance style with a sundial engraved on the south wall.

Before investigating the rest of its history and architecture look at the arms on the font — and hear a story. Those are the arms of Sir John Gayer, a Cornishman and merchant adventurer who became Lord Mayor of London. One day, when travelling in a caravan of merchants through Arabia, he became isolated from the band as the sun was setting and was beset by lions. Gayer went down on his knees and prayed for protection, offering all the profits from his venture if he should be spared. He opened his eyes, and a lion crouched ready to spring turned about and ran off.

Sir John, impressed by this sign of Divine intervention, left a large sum of money to the poor of this parish, provided that the 'Lion Sermon' is preached annually on the anniversary of his death.

Baltic Exchange

St Mary Axe connects Leadenhall Street with Houndsditch. Halfway down it is the Baltic Mercantile and Shipping Exchange. Though its building dates from 1903 the exchange finds its origin in far earlier times. R. J. Blackham in *The Sovereign City* explains 'On a site now occupied by the Post Office once stood a coffee house known as the Baltic, whose proprietor . . . placed a room at the disposal of the merchants concerned with the importation of produce from countries surrounding the Baltic Sea . . . chiefly of tallow, skins and hemp.' That was in the eighteenth century.

Meanwhile shipowners, brokers and merchants in the Eastern trade had formed their own fraternity at the Old Jerusalem Coffee House. It came about that two allied interests were looking for better accommodation; happily they agreed to pool their resources and combine in the effort to have a 'handsome new Exchange erected' in 1903. With restoration and enlargement in 1956 it now houses some 700 member companies operating under the motto, 'Our word, our bond', which means that a great volume of business is still effected by word of mouth and mutual trust.

St Helen's, Bishopsgate

Turn off from Bishopsgate under the archway which leads to Great St Helen's and there is a little oasis of calm round St Helen's where the tide of traffic has ebbed away from the churchyard. A seat invites a pause for thought, perhaps of the score of important people immortalized within by fine memorials, from the brasses of the fifteenth century to the altar tomb of Sir Thomas Gresham (see Royal Exchange) who died in 1579. William Kent, in *London for Everyman* claims St Helen's as 'one of the oldest and most interesting of the City churches'. It is said on doubtful authority that the Emperor Constantine had it built to honour his mother Empress Helena who died some time in the fourth century. Records show that there was a church here in 1140. An arch and the lancet windows are of the following century, with the two eastern chapels added in the fourteenth century and the arcade and roofs a hundred years later.

The fact that it escaped the 1666 Fire allowed the preservation of that early architecture as a whole, as well as all those monuments, one of which, that to Sir William Pickering, has been adjudged the finest in any City church. On a pillar can be seen the carved stand, decorated with the arms of the City and of Charles II, which at that time was attached to the Lord Mayor's pew to serve as rest for the sword and mace, the symbols of his office.

Leathersellers' Hall

When the ancient nunnery which stood in Great St Helen's was relieved of its possessions by Henry VIII, the Leathersellers' Company bought their house and used the refectory as its Livery Hall until 1799, when it was so far beyond repair that it was demolished in favour of a purpose-built Hall. In 1878 it was rebuilt and further extended in 1926, as befitted one of the wealthiest City livery companies, incorporated as early as 1444. Then came the 1939 War, and severe fire damage in the Blitz, but yet again the Leathersellers put their home to rights, over ten years from 1949, to the design of Kenneth Peacock.

A surprising feature outside the Hall, with its beautiful coat of arms so proudly displayed, is a huge steel turntable let into the street at the end of the cul-de-sac called St Helen's Place. It was installed before the last war so that those early, influential motorists might arrive and depart without having to experience the difficulty of turning or reversing in the narrow street.

St Ethelburga, Bishopsgate

The dedication celebrates the daughter of King Ethelbert, the first Saxon ruler to become a Christian, so it is not surprising that it claims to be the earliest church in London. It is also the smallest, being but sixty feet by thirty. Certainly its frontage to Bishopsgate is minute, with a worn stone porch beneath a stumpy tower which supports a timber bell cote and a weathervane wrought in iron to show the date 1671, although the cote itself is of the following century. The church building dates from 1400 and was lucky enough to escape the great conflagration of 2 September 1666. On 19 April 1607, Henry Hudson came here with his eleven-man crew to receive communion before their voyage in search of the North-West Passage to the 'islands of spicery'. His daring and his dreadful fate in a later voyage are recorded in three stained-glass windows designed by Leonard Walker and inserted between 1928 and 1930, midway through the incumbency of the unconventional and much-loved W. F. Geikie-Cobb who is remembered in a window on the north side.

St Botolph Aldgate

George Dance, the Elder, architect of the Mansion House, designed this church when it was rebuilt in 1741 in dark red brick with stone quoins to its apertures. It had to be restored again between 1966 and 1971 after damage by fire. In the unusual octagonal vestibule is the font, with its original cover, delightfully domed in the manner of a little temple. Here the monuments older than the church have been placed. Thomas Darcy and Sir Nicholas Carew, beheaded on Tower Hill in 1538, Robert Dow, who died in 1612, and Sir John Cass, founder in 1710 of the nearby Sir John Cass Foundation School are represented.

Other famous people associated with St Botolph's include Daniel Defoe, married in the former church in 1683 and Jeremy Bentham, writer on jurisprudence and ethics, who was baptised in the new church in 1747. Thomas Bray, founder of the S.P.C.K. and the S.P.G., was vicar here from 1708 until his death in 1730. He was also a pioneer of the public library movement, having established one hundred and nineteen parochial libraries in Britain and America.

St Botolph-without-Bishopsgate

All around the hallowed ground the windows of towering office blocks catch the sun and dazzle the eye, making the interior of St Botolph's cooler, quieter, that much more inviting. The church was rebuilt in 1728, to James Gold's design, and is unique in the City in having its tower at the east end. At the existing font John Keats was baptised in 1795. A chapel has been set aside for remembrance of the Honourable Artillery Company and the London Rifle Brigade also keeps its Book of Remembrance here.

A simple 'remembrance' of those men who have served the parish from its inception is the picking out in letters of gold of their names and dates in a line which runs all round just under the gallery. An inscription explains, 'The names of the Rectors were inserted April 1864 . . . and they truly were many priests because they were not suffered to continue by reason of death. (Hebrews VII 23, 24.)'

Every windowsill has a tablet on it engraved with a list of names. One sill gives the reason, 'To perpetuate the memory of the benefactors of the poor of this parish the trustees of the parish estates have placed a marble tablet in the recesses of each window . . . August 1873.' Just down the street a golden mitre high up on the buildings on both sides of the street shows where Bishop's Gate once stood — and gave its name to the church.

Dirty Dick's

Opposite Liverpool Street Station, on the other side of Bishopsgate, stands Dirty Dick's Wine House, its modern façade preserving the effigy of Dirty Dick in his blue coat. The entrance to the saloon bar is down the narrow Swedeland Court, where the atmosphere is of an earlier age. It claims to have been established as early as 1745 when Dirty Dick, whose real name was Nathaniel Bentley, was but a boy, son of a well-to-do ironmonger in Leadenhall Street who died in 1761. Nathaniel enjoyed his inheritance, dressed in the height of fashion and spent lavishly, arranging a great banquet to celebrate his engagement to a beautiful woman. She died on that very day and he ordered the room to be shut up with the feast set out; it was not opened again until he died.

Meanwhile he went about unwashed, uncombed and uncaring, called 'Dirty Dick' by all the children, until he died in 1809 and the room was opened to reveal the remnants of that feast with the addition of skeletons of dead mice and rats. The enterprising landlord of a tavern in Bishopsgate bought up these pathetic remains, installed them in his tavern, and drew crowds of interested customers so that eventually the place itself became known as 'Dirty Dick's'.

Spitalfields

Though its physical location is just outside the city, Spitalfields market is owned and controlled by the Corporation of the City of London and thus merits inclusion in this book. It is a mere step over the City boundary down Brushfield Street or Spital Square, but it has to be a very early step for the sightseer because trading, from Monday through to Saturday, starts at four in the morning.

Following a charter granted by Charles II in 1682, Spitalfields developed into the present wholesale fruit, vegetable and flower market. It was privately owned right up to 1920, when the Corporation bought it and spent two million pounds on modernization and enlargement from three to five acres before having the new buildings opened by Queen Mary in 1928. The London Fruit Exchange was completed a year later and in 1935 a new flower market was opened, so that today the main market frontage extends over a mile and a half, some 180 wholesale merchants are represented, and over 2,000 people are employed.

The good monks who built the Priory of St Mary Spital back in 1197 would be greatly surprised if they could see the present-day traffic and bustle in their fair fields.

Finsbury Circus

All around, from Moorgate to Liverpool Street, the traffic thunders on, but in the green heart of Finsbury Circus a leaking tap on the drinking fountain adds drop by quiet drop to the pool on the path in which the sparrows slake their thirst. How exciting it is to find in the middle of these tree-shaded gardens such a reminder of childhood fun and refreshment, and one that is still working, having been provided by the Metropolitan Drinking Fountain and Cattle Trough Association in 1902. The hasp from which the original metal cup hung on a chain can still be seen. The gardens are a welcome refuge from the City's bustle, and the bowls roll peacefully over the close-cropped green, overlooked by many grand buildings including Lutyens' (1869-1944) Britannic House.

The original Moorgate, built in 1415 and demolished in 1761, was situated to the southwest at the junction with London Wall. It gave on to the marshy ground outside the old Roman wall where Moorfields now runs, and where archers then practised and washerwomen put out their clothes to dry.

Liverpool Street Station

The tide of human beings that surges in and out of this railway station every day finds its way, like water, through every entrance and exit. Many of those hurrying feet never touch the floor of the main station approach. Their owners miss a view of the station buildings, erected in 1875, which is most pleasing, especially when the setting sun makes the yellow brickwork glow; and they miss, too, the moving stories told by the memorials in the main Booking Hall.

In the centre of the left-hand wall a huge tablet is inscribed, 'To the glory of God and in grateful memory of those members of the Great Eastern Railway staff who, in response to the call of their King and country, sacrificed their lives during the Great War'. There must be at least 1300 names appended, and each one of them an individual with his own tragic story, his own all-too-short existence. Nearer to the platform is a monument to Field-Marshal Sir Henry Wilson who died on Thursday 22 June 1922 within two hours of unveiling that memorial! Nearer the street, another plaque has been placed to the memory of Captain Charles Fryatt, master of the Great Eastern Railway's ship *Brussels*. He had kept the route to neutral Holland open, dodging the German submarines, but on 27 July 1916 he was captured by a German destroyer and shot the same day.

Key to Location Map

1. Victoria Embankment
2. The Temple
3. The Temple Church
4. Temple Bar 1
5. Temple Bar 2
6. St Dunstan-in-the-West
7. Fleet Street
8. Johnson's House
9. Wine Office Court
10. Ye Olde Cheshire Cheese
11. Salisbury Court
12. St Bride's Church
13. St Bride Foundation Institute
14. Blackfriars Bridge
15. St Andrew-by-the-Wardrobe
16. Apothecaries' Hall
17. St Benet's Church
18. College of Arms
19. The Bell, Carter Lane
20. Painters' Hall
21. Beaver House
22. Vintners' Hall
23. Southwark Bridge
24. St Michael, Paternoster Royal
25. Skinners' Hall
26. Fishmongers' Hall
27. London Bridge
28. The Monument
29. Billingsgate
30. Custom House
31. St Dunstan-in-the-East
32. Baker's Hall
33. Tower of London 1
34. Tower of London 2
35. Tower of London 3
36. Tower of London 4
37. Tower Bridge
38. Tower Hill
39. All Hallows-by-the-Tower
40. Trinity House
41. Corn Exchange
42. St Olave's, Hart Street
43. Lloyd's 1
44. Lloyd's 2
45. Fenchurch Street Station
46. All Hallows, Staining
47. St Margaret Pattens
48. Leadenhall Market
49. London Metal Exchange
50. St Peter-Upon-Cornhill
51. St Michael's Alley
52. Lombard Street
53. St Edmund, The King & Martyr
54. Mansion House
55. St Stephen, Walbrook
56. St Mary Abchurch
57. Temple of Mithras
58. Poultry
59. Mercers' Hall
60. Bow Church
61. Ye Olde Watling
62. Panyer Alley Steps
63. St Paul's Churchyard 1
64. St Paul's Churchyard 2
65. St Paul's Cathedral 1
66. St Paul's Cathedral 2
67. St Paul's Cathedral 3
68. St Martin-within-Ludgate
69. Stationers' Hall
70. Amen Court
71. Cutlers' Hall
72. Newgate Street
73. Old Bailey
74. Church of the Holy Sepulchre
75. Holborn Viaduct
76. The City Temple
77. St Andrew's Holborn
78. Holborn Circus
79. Staple Inn
80. Smithfield 1
81. Smithfield 2
82. St Bartholomew-the-Great 1
83. St Bartholomew-the-Great 2
84. St Bartholomew's Hospital
85. The Fat Boy
86. Penny Post
87. Butchers' Hall
88. Museum of London
89. London Wall
90. Barbican
91. St Giles', Cripplegate
92. St Alphage
93. Pewterers' Hall
94. Haberdashers' Hall
95. Goldsmiths' Hall
96. St Mary Aldermanbury
97. Guildhall 1
98. Guildhall 2
99. Guildhall 3
100. Guildhall Library
101. St Lawrence Jewry
102. St Margaret Lothbury
103. Bank of England
104. Threadneedle Street
105. Royal Exchange 1
106. Royal Exchange 2
107. Stock Exchange
108. St Andrew Undershaft
109. St Katharine Cree
110. Baltic Exchange
111. St Helen's, Bishopsgate
112. Leathersellers' Hall
113. St Ethelburga, Bishopsgate
114. St Botolph Aldgate
115. St Botolph-without-Bishopsgate
116. Dirty Dick's
117. Spitalfields
118. Finsbury Circus
119. Liverpool Street Station

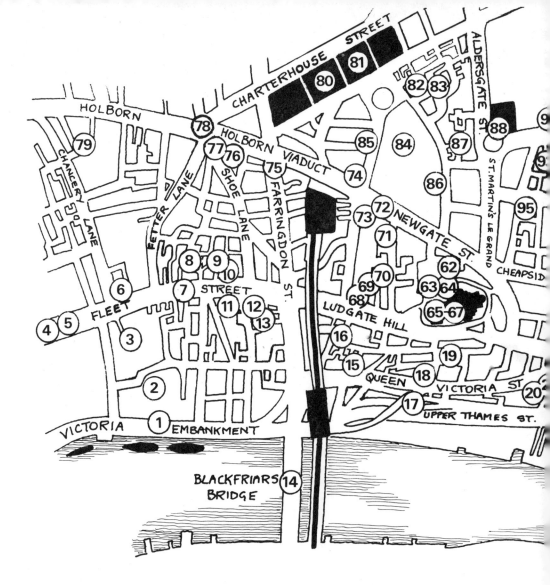

City of London

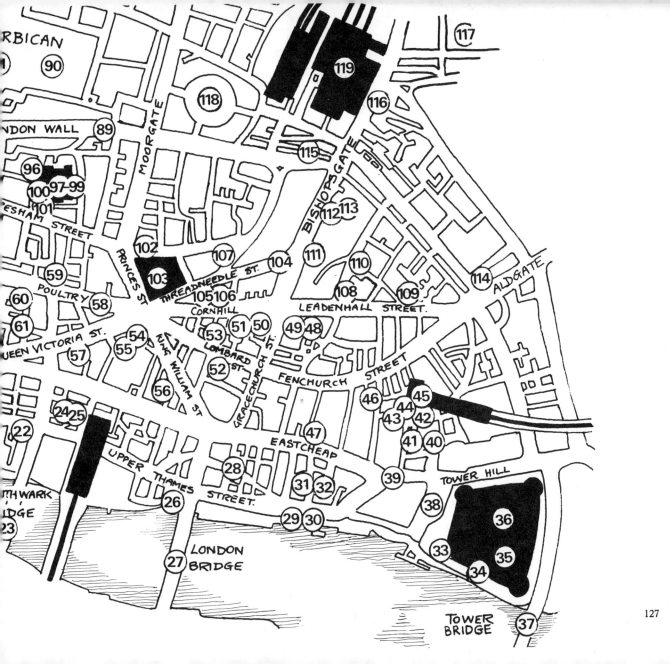